Children and Babies with Mood Swings

New Insights for Parents and Professionals

D1531495

Stanley I. Greenspan, M.D.

and

Ira Glovinsky, Ph.D.

with

Cindy Glovinsky, M.S.W.

Table of Contents

INTRODUCTION

A New Understanding of the Development of Mood Swings and How Children Learn to Regulate Their Emotions and Behaviors

In recent years, our research group has had a unique opportunity to study how infants and young children develop their minds and brains. In particular we have explored how they develop their emotional and social capacities, including their ability to experience moods. Even more importantly, we have identified how they develop their ability to regulate or control them. Through observing large numbers of infants and young children developing, we have arrived at a new understanding of mood swings in children and of the ways in which both parents and professionals can help children learn to experience their moods, comprehend them and regulate or control them. This understanding transcends the classic division of biological vs. environmental by looking at children's mood swings within the broader context of emotional development.

One of the missing pieces in our understanding of mood swings has been the early developmental pathways that led to these patterns. We believe that certain twists and turns on the route to adulthood may often be associated with mood swings or bipolar "roller coaster" mood patterns, and in this book we show how this works in detail. We also share some new insights about how children can learn to more fully experience, regulate, and control their moods and we provide a guide for both parents and professionals to help children use their emotions to further healthy growth and development.

As we all know, emotions are a two-way street: they enable us to love, cooperate, and have empathy or compassion, but they can also overwhelm us, fuel impulsive behavior, or lead to depression. The key is to become aware of, to interpret, and to regulate our emotions so that we can make use of them in furthering our humanity. We explore these ideas about mood swings in children through a series of stories/case presentations about children and their development and their challenges in the chapters that follow. In Chapter 1, we describe Freddy, a child with a bipolar mood pattern, and present a model which describes the developmental pathways associated with this pattern. This model can help us to understand and intervene to help children like Freddy earlier and more successfully. In Chapters 2 and 3 we meet two more children, Carla and Jimmy, and describe how we, as professionals, have worked with these children and their families to shape the developmental pathways associated with their mood swings and to provide them with the comprehensive programs— which include therapy, psychiatric medications, parent guidance, and school interventions—that they need.

Before describing these cases, however, we want to explain briefly how children's moods and emotional interactions develop. Infants and young children begin experiencing more and more complex emotions throughout the first year of life, and by the end of the first year—and into the early part of the second year—they are already experiencing emotions in terms of patterns. We observe, for example, happy moods and sad moods and angry moods or irritable moods in our just-walking little toddlers. Interestingly, we have discovered that our adventuresome toddlers are at the same time discovering that their caregivers have emotional patterns too. They're already sensing when Daddy is grumpy, when Mommy is happy and likely to give them an extra cookie, and when their sibling is about to crash down on them and take their favorite toy. During this time, we increasingly see emotional interactions between infants/toddlers and their caregivers, and these interactions shape how effectively children learn to deal with their emotions. Some interactions with caregivers help children learn to regulate and enjoy their emotions, while others accentuate the intensity of the emotions to such a degree that they undermine healthy development and lead to more extreme or dysregulated mood states, including impulsive, agitated, or depressed patterns.

Some toddlers and caregivers become engaged in interactions where there is a wonderful balance in the way they use emotions to communicate. For example, as the toddler begins to get a slightly frustrated look in his eyes and seems two steps away from a tantrum, Mommy senses the child's emerging feeling and shifts into a soothing voice, saying, "Are you trying to reach this little, bright red car here? Huh? Huh?" As Mommy speaks, the already slightly relieved toddler, hearing the warmth and empathy in her voice, motions, still angrily, with his hands a "Yes!" while making a gruff sound indicating that he's tired of waiting. Hearing this, Mommy is even more soothing in her tone of voice, her facial expression, and her body posture, as she reaches out to move the car a bit closer, asking, "Can I help, Sweetheart? Can I help?" A bit relieved, our impatient toddler nods yes, pointing to the desired red car. Mom, wanting to challenge her little guy while soothing and helping him, nods, "Here it comes!" and puts it within his reach but not in his hand so he can experience the mastery of going to get it at the same time that he's been experiencing her soothing, empathetic help. The result: a tantrum has been averted. More importantly, successful, shared problem-solving has been experienced and, even more importantly, our little toddler has learned a social interaction in which he has used his emotions to communicate with his mommy and Mommy has used her emotions to communicate back.

Or consider a toddler looking a bit preoccupied and sad and not showing any interest in his toys. His dad, who is sitting on the floor next to him, senses the lack of enthusiasm and becomes more playful, energizing up his voice a bit. Perhaps Dad recognized that he had been a bit preoccupied thinking about work while playing with his son, resulting in the toddler losing interest. Now, with great enthusiasm, Dad gestures to his son to push the car toward him so he can do something funny with it. Dad demonstrates by pressing on the car so it makes a fun noise, lights up, and moves. As Dad continues to talk about how much fun this is in his energized voice, little Johnny tries it and breaks into a big smile at the results. Dad continues to play interactively with more energy and enthusiasm and gets into a wonderful rhythm of back-and-forth interactions with Johnny, pushing cars and balls. He eventually explores the rest of the room together with his little son. In this example, Dad responded to Johnny's lack of enthusiasm with more playful, energized emotion on his part and pulled his little toddler into a joyful interaction. In both these examples, we observe a pattern of emotional interaction that we describe as "counter-regulation" or "counter-balancing."

In this special pattern of emotional interaction, the caregiver reads—and responds to—the child's emotional cues in a way that counter-regulates or counter-balances what the child is experiencing. This helps the child use his emotions to communicate and feel regulated, calmed, and masterful rather than disorganized and dysregulated. Over literally thousands of such interactions occurring each week, our toddlers and children learn to experience and regulate their emotions and to employ them for positive social relationships and healthy development.

We've also observed the opposite pattern. Here, as our toddler begins to express his annoyance with an angry look, a gruff sound, and an annoyed finger-pointing towards the red car, the caregiver responds with equal annoyance, and in a slightly annoyed vocal tone says, "You'd better wait!" As our assertive little toddler ups the stakes and his pointed finger turns into a hand banging on the floor, demanding the red car that he's eyeing, his caregiver ups the stakes as well and, in a very annoyed voice, bordering on anger, says, "No banging here!" Not to be intimidated, our toddler hits one of the caregiver's favorite lamps, leading the caregiver to yell, which, in turn, frightens even our assertive little guy and, within seconds, he's throwing one of his more aggressive fits by banging the floor and pushing at his caregiver as she comes near him. Angry with her little toddler, our caregiver then tells him he's going to have to have a time-out and a few minutes later, after no social interaction, we see him either further agitated or looking solemn, sad, and despondent. Over a period of weeks, with this pattern repeated many times, his tantrums, agitation, and bouts of sadness increase in frequency, intensity, and duration. As this pattern is repeated thousands of times each week, we observe children developing more and more extreme mood swings, and, as a consequence, more family stress and challenges. Not infrequently we observe impulsivity/aggression and agitation and/or sadness and depression.

Another pattern contributing to mood swings, more on the sad or depressive end of the continuum, is when the child experiments with some assertiveness or perhaps even aggression and the caregiver, for whatever reason—sometimes anxiety—pulls in his or her emotions so there is a quality of an emptiness or empty space in place of a vibrant and continuing emotional interchange. The toddler or young child may experience this as an empty feeling and a loss. Repeated over many times, the child comes to associate her own assertiveness or experimentation or curiosity with loss and emptiness and we may see more sadness or depressive tendencies as development proceeds. This scenario can play out at older ages as well.

In children who are learning to regulate their emotions and use them for social interactions and mastery, we also frequently see caregiver-child interactions at a slightly older age in which caregivers and preschoolers are involved in pretend play with one another. In these interactions, the dollies or action figures have feelings and are exchanging expressions of happiness or sadness or excitement through words or actions or dramas involving exploration, discovery, power, grandeur, control, caution, or fear. Through grand epics of make-believe play, the child's inner world of emotion is now being expressed to the child herself as well as to her caregivers. These elaborate pretend dramas embrace the major emotions of life and enable the child to develop a verbal or symbolic understanding of the human emotional terrain. The caregiver and child are experiencing this emotional terrain in a pleasurable, social, calm, and regulated manner. As the child becomes even older, she uses this verbal understanding with a supportive, empathetic caregiver to logically explore her feelings and can tell the caregiver why she feels happy or sad or angry. She can look at the many reasons for her feelings and understand that they occur in various shades of gray as she begins to get beyond all-or-nothing or extreme emotional states. Eventually, with regulating and supportive caregiving, she can learn to evaluate her own moods and by the early teenage years say things such as "Gee, I was angrier than usual" or "I wonder why I'm feeling irritable today, it's not my typical pattern."

For the child who starts off with a dysregulated mood or mood swings, each of these steps—from fantasy play to logical explanations to understanding the shades of gray to evaluating his own feelings—is more difficult, especially if the caregiving pattern keeps accentuating rather than counter-balancing the child's mood. The constructive pattern, therefore, involves reading and responding to the child's emotional cues, maintaining a continuous flow of back-and-forth emotional interactions characterized by shared regulation, counter-balancing, calm, regulated fantasy play, logical discussion of feelings, exploration of the subtleties or gradations of feelings, and support for self-evaluation. The maladaptive pattern—the one leading to greater and greater mood swings—is characterized by misreading the child's emotional cues; accentuating rather than counter-balancing the child's emotional states; only intermittent rather than continuous back-and-forth social interactions; action-oriented rather than fantasy play; emphasis on punishment or consequences rather than an equal emphasis on understanding the reasons for feeling; maintenance of extreme or polarized feeling states rather than an appreciation of the subtleties or gradations of feelings; and lack of support for self-evaluation.

These insights about the development of either healthy emotional regulation or greater and greater mood swings are only part of the puzzle we've been able to explore. The other part involves the biology of mood swings. There is a great deal of evidence that people with extreme mood swings, including bipolar patterns, evidence genetic and biological differences. What we've realized however, is that these genetic differences do not express themselves directly in mood swings, but influence the way the baby and the toddler experience routine sensations such as touch, sound, smell, taste, and their own movement patterns. We've observed a unique constellation of biological differences that are expressed during development. These include a tendency for infants and toddlers to be very reactive to sensations such as touch and sound. This, in turn, makes it easier for the infant or toddler to be more easily overwhelmed. A loud noise, an angry tone of voice from Mom or Dad, or what seems to the caregiver to be a firm touch may all be experienced by the toddler as an overwhelming assault. Tantrums or agitation thereby become more easily precipitated. Some of these differences have been described as temperamental differences, but we've been able to trace them to the way a child experiences basic sensations such as touch and sound.

Another part of this biological puzzle that separates the child with mood swings from the child who is just cautious or inhibited is that a child prone to mood swings, when he is overwhelmed, typically switches gears and becomes physically active and seems to seek out the very sensations which overwhelm him. He becomes what is described as "sensory seeking," continually getting involved in situations which are overwhelming to him.

As might be imagined, the more extreme this biological tendency is towards over-reactivity coupled with hyperactivity and sensory seeking, the more difficult it is for caregivers to engage in reading or responding to the child's emotional cues, counter-regulating, fantasy play, logical exploration of feelings, and higher levels of reflective thinking about feelings. Therefore, the more extreme the child's biology, the more help caregivers need to provide for the child to maintain healthy patterns. We illustrate how this task can be accomplished and, importantly, how it's never too late to institute it.

Children's mood swings have perplexed parents and professionals for thousands of years. Explanations and strategies for responding to these mood swings, however, have varied over the centuries. In general, there has been an ebb and flow between biological, brain-based explanations and more psychological explanations and approaches based on the belief that mood swings are learned behaviors that could be controlled with proper education. Many of the treatments historically prescribed for moodiness would, by today's standards, be considered superstitious rather than science-based.

Our modern understanding of children's mood swings has unfortunately repeated some of the shifts in the history of this distinctly human pattern. Even in relatively recent times, there is still a division between professionals advocating strictly biochemical explanations and treatments and those advocating educational and/or psychological ones. Some claim that extreme mood swings are disorders of the brain due to genetic and biochemical irregularities while others attribute them to upbringing, education, and other aspects of the environment. Meanwhile, a certain proportion of our children continue to exhibit a full range of mood problems, from everyday mood shifts and misbehavior to routine prolonged bouts of sadness to major bouts of depression or agitation and impulsivity. These are described as the children's version of bipolar disorder.

Descriptions of children's mood swings have a long history. In psychiatric journals, countless articles have appeared describing children who spend their lives on an emotional roller coaster characterized by both extreme "ups" and extreme "downs." Their mood swings and associated behaviors range from everyday challenges such as a child having a tantrum because she can't get her way to major, prolonged bouts of irritability, quickened speech, unrealistic and often grandiose thinking, and impulsive, even dangerous behavior alternating with extremes of depression and despondency. During these episodes, even young children say "I wish I were never born," "I shouldn't be alive," or "Everything I do is wrong." Understanding how these feelings and behaviors develop provides a new approach to helping children in families.

Often, parents and professionals have questions about the role of medication in helping a child to overcome his mood swings. Given our developmental perspective concerning the pathways leading through the mood swings to the healthy regulation of moods, we would say that medication may have a role for selected children, but not as a treatment in its own right. It may be a piece of the comprehensive program to foster better regulation and mastery of the developmental steps outlined earlier.

Before continuing, we need to clarify the terms we use in this book. We use the term "children with mood swings" rather than any standard diagnostic term to describe children with mood fluctuation patterns. In some children, mood swings are revealed mainly through irritability, aggression, negativism, or impulsivity and distractibility. In others, they may be revealed through lots of experiences with sadness, a lack of energy and interest in expected activities, self-critical comments, or many expressions of hopelessness or helplessness. Many children go from one state to the other, but each child with mood swings has his or her own unique mood profile.

Children whose moods are most intense and who swing from one extreme to the other are often described as having "bipolar patterns." Many professionals have expressed disagreement on whether children should be diagnosed with bipolar disorder and if the childhood version of this problem is on a continuum with the adult version. We sometimes use the term "bipolar patterns" to describe children who vary between the two extremes described here. For example, it's not unusual for a child who behaves aggressively or impulsively to subsequently feel remorseful and despondent, even hopeless. We take the position that whether or not children with extreme mood swings should be seen as having bipolar *disorder* or simply bipolar type *patterns,* it's essential that the children receive the proper help to learn to regulate their moods and feel better about themselves. The ability to engage in relationships and age-expected activities in a positive, stable, and optimistic manner is vital for healthy development. When we discuss the clinical cases, as well as the history and some of the important research on children with mood swings, including those who are described as having bipolar patterns, we sometimes use these terms interchangeably or mention both mood swings and bipolar patterns. We do this to emphasize that, from a developmental point of view, mood swings and their different forms, including bipolar patterns, are all part of a developmental process that we need to help children master.

In summary, our research with infants and young children has provided a unique window into the development of moods, including mood swings. It has highlighted the significance of emotional signaling as a pivotal step in human development. If emotional signaling can be used for social interaction and regulating moods, behaviors and thoughts, a child is on a healthy developmental pathway. If, on the other hand, emotions are not developed to the point of being used as signals and, because of the child's biology, are not harnessed by caregivers for the goal of social signaling and regulation, the child may remain instead in an earlier, more catastrophic form (all-or-nothing expression). Then we often see greater and greater mood swings and compromises in the steps of healthy development.

CHAPTER 1

A Case of a Child with a Bipolar Pattern of Mood Dysregulation

Children with cyclic patterns of extreme "ups" and "downs" present unique challenges to parents and professionals alike. They often evidence many different biological and psychological difficulties—and strengths—within the context of complex family patterns. The developmental pathways leading to these difficulties can be hard to trace. Thus, it can be helpful to construct a model that summarizes the patterns that unfold as a child develops. This model describes the case of Freddy, a "typical" child with a bipolar pattern of mood dysregulation. This is not a real case, but a composite of many children with similar problems.

From the beginning, psychodynamic psychotherapy with children and their families—as well as with adults—has been based on such models, as clinicians sought to better understand human development. A long history of developmental insights has contributed to this foundation, including the works of Sigmund Freud, Anna Freud, Margaret Mahler, D.W. Winnicott, Eric Erikson, Hans Kohut, and John Bowlby as well as more recent research and clinical work with infants and families.

Our model of children with mood swings, including bipolar patterns, is rooted in a more general, comprehensive model of child development based on our clinical work dealing with a wide variety of challenges in infants and children. This model, which builds on the models of our predecessors,is called the Developmental, Individual-Difference, Relationship-Based (DIR) model.[1] It provides an additional lens through which we may look not only at the content of early life, such as walking, talking, or toilet training, for example, but

---

[1]For more information about the DIR model, please see www.floortime.org.

also at the psychological and biological structures developing during the early years. The DIR model emphasizes three components that help the clinician assess and treat the child:

1. **Functional emotional developmental stages:** In the course of their development, children must acquire certain skills at certain stages that have to do with thinking, feeling, and communicating. These include the ability to pay attention; to regulate their moods (calm themselves); to engage in a two-way interaction; to communicate feelings by means of gestures; to engage in long chains of two-way interactions in which caregiver and child work together to calm the child and solve problems; to form internal images of wishes, intentions, and feelings; and to build logical bridges between these images.

2. **Individual sensory processing differences:** Children have many different ways of processing the information they take in through their five senses. Some are easily overwhelmed by sensory information, while others respond only to extreme stimuli. Different children may favor different sensory channels and may have different difficulties understanding what they perceive.

3. **Child-caregiver relationships:** These include not only relationships with caregivers after the child can speak, but gestural interactions as well. In both pre-verbal and verbal relationships, what is important is how feelings are communicated.

Freddy's case shows how the DIR model enables us to identify possible early differences in the way sensory information is processed and early developmental patterns that may lead to extreme moods, and to put together a comprehensive program that takes these developmental differences into account.

Clinicians in recent years have become increasingly interested in early identification and clinical work with bipolar patterns in children. In children with rollercoaster moods, sadness or despondency often vacillates with aggression or agitation rather than with the frantic, grandiose mania that causes bipolar adults to stay up all night calling friends or spend their whole life savings in a single uncontrolled shopping spree. While the presence of mania in adults defines bipolarity, some aggression, agitation, and irritability may be symptomatic of many different disorders in children. This makes diagnosis difficult.

Nor are there any clear indicators that a child is likely to develop bipolar disorder. A host of possible deficits—including language, motor, perceptual, attention, executive functioning, and social delays—have been suggested as possible signs that a child might become bipolar, but no definitive pattern of characteristics has yet been identified.

Because diagnosis of bipolar patterns is difficult, treatment methods are currently less developed for extreme moodiness than for most other types of childhood problems. So far, treatment for bipolar patterns has mainly involved medications, especially mood-stabilizers such as lithium. Psychotherapy for children with mood swings is in its infancy, and no comprehensive intervention program that incorporates interpersonal, family, and educational elements has been developed.

The case we are about to describe suggests a novel theory about what leads to certain children's rollercoaster moods. This involves all three of the components of the DIR model: functional emotional developmental stages, individual sensory processing differences, and child-caregiver relationships. The case also illustrates the type of comprehensive program needed to help children with bipolar patterns.

Freddy is biologically at risk for bipolarity not because of just one characteristic, but because of an atypical combination of three:

1. **Hypersensitivity plus sensory-craving:** Extra-moody children tend to be hypersensitive, especially to sound and touch, but they respond differently to sensory overload than other hypersensitive children do. Most hypersensitive children become fearful and avoidant when their senses are overloaded, but children with bipolar patterns become quite the opposite: they crave *more* sensations, not less, preferably involving motion, high activity, aggression, agitation, and impulsivity. The more overwhelmed they feel, the faster they run around and the more furiously they strike out in all directions, which results in even more sensory overload. Thus, they become caught in a vicious circle of sensory overload and hypersensitivity that feed into one another.

2. **Difficulties co-regulating with caregivers:** From early infancy, the majority of children and their caregivers work together in their interactions to co-regulate the child's mood—to either calm down the agitated child or cheer up the despondent child through emotionally sensitive back-and-forth exchanges. In children with bipolar patterns, these exchanges are incomplete, leaving the child with a deficit in mood regulation.

3. **Difficulty thinking about feelings:** The rollercoaster child's mind contains few internal pictures or other representations of feelings, which are thus more likely to be acted out or expressed in disguised form through physical symptoms. Feelings may also be split, or polarized into extreme opposites that are experienced one at a time by turns, first love, then hate, for example, rather than as a complex mixture.

Freddy's case also illustrates family patterns that may further increase the risk of bipolar mood dysregulation. Dr. G.'s job is to help the family—as well as teachers and other professionals—to cope more effectively with the child's difficulties and thus reduce this risk.

Case of a Child with Mood Dysregulation

Freddy was nine years old when he came in with his parents for an evaluation with Dr. G. He lived at home with his mother, father, six-year-old sister, and four-year-old brother. Freddy's parents were worried because he was frequently "losing control" with his two younger siblings. He would yell and scream and often hit them when they came into his room. When his parents, Mr. and Ms. B., tried to scold or discipline him—Mr. B. prided himself on being a firm disciplinarian—Freddy would become remorseful and say he wished he were dead and that it would be better if he were never born. He also talked about jumping out of his second story bedroom window.

Such behavior confused Freddy's parents. Sometimes Freddy could be happy, cooperative, and "talk about everyday things." However, at other times (and this was becoming *most* of the time), Freddy would either become angry—blaming his siblings, parents, and teachers for his "foul mood"—or depressed, escapist, and avoidant. His spells of "losing it" were getting worse, with tantrums that lasted an hour or two. At times, Mr. B. even had to restrain him—for example, when he went for knives in the kitchen, threatening to stab his brother.

Freddy's teacher reported that at school he tended to blame others for his problems, complaining that the other kids were "being unfair" and were "all out to get me." Sometimes he would fight with and hurt another child by hitting him in the face, and at other times he would talk sadly about wanting to leave school. "Everyone would be better off without me," he would tell his teacher. As a result, Freddy had no close friends and the other children were shying further and further away from him.

Academically, Freddy had both strengths and weaknesses. He was highly verbal and a good reader but found it hard, in spite of his good ideas, to actually write things down. He had difficulties with math, which was his weakest subject. His penmanship, overall coordination, and athletic skills were also weak. Cognitively, he appeared stronger at remembering details and weaker at seeing the big picture.

Freddy's parents described a developmental history characterized by precocious language development and slower, though still normal, motor development. Freddy had been emotionally sensitive, reactive and moody since infancy. Until age eight, however, he had not behaved aggressively or made worrisome threats to hurt himself. Then, shortly before Freddy began to have serious problems, two factors changed: Ms. B. became preoccupied with her sister, who had become seriously ill, and Freddy began finding school work more difficult, especially math.

A few months before our evaluation, a child psychiatrist had diagnosed Freddy with ADHD. A workup by a clinical psychologist led to a diagnosis of conduct disorder. Subsequently, a second child psychiatrist raised the possibility that Freddy had bipolar disorder, based on Freddy's behavior as well as a family history of depression and an uncle whom Mr. and Ms. B. described as both grandiose and impulsive. Mr. B. appeared to be an intense, driven person, prone to angry outbursts, but he had never had a formal psychiatric diagnosis. Ms. B. seemed anxious and depressed and had been in psychotherapy in the past. Freddy's parents were now seeking a fourth evaluation because a brief trial with Ritalin had made him even more agitated than he was before. They were dissatisfied with the help they had received in the past and wanted to learn what they could do and how Mr. B. especially could learn to cope more effectively with his son. They were reluctant to try additional medications and hoped the right therapy would make this unnecessary.

When Freddy came in for his interview, Dr. G. encountered a well-groomed nine-year-old who immediately looked him over and struck up a conversation, commenting on toys and games around the room. He began talking quickly about school, the other children, and people being unfair to him. He said he knew why he was there—because he had hit his brother and sister. But, as he explained it, "they deserved it and they should be the ones having to talk to someone." Freddy went on to describe in great detail various incidents that had occurred at home. These incidents always had a common theme of someone invading his space, usually his brother or sister, but often also his father, who could be intrusive. Freddy described his mother as more protective but as favoring the younger children and "forcing my hand."

Freddy seemed able to talk indirectly about his feelings, but not directly, using "feeling words." When Dr. G. asked what things were like at school, for example, Freddy volunteered that a lot of kids picked on him and complained that this wasn't fair. Although he would look sad and talk about not being wanted, he never said the word "sad." It was as if he did not have that word in his vocabulary. Likewise, when Freddy began to feel angry talking about his parents and siblings, he never used the word "angry" to describe his feelings, but instead bragged excitedly about how he had hit, pushed, or pulled someone out of his room.

During the interview, Freddy's mood seemed to swing from mild agitation to sadness, emotional hunger, and neediness. When he was agitated, he darted around the room and jumped from subject to subject. When Freddy was calm and looked sad—about half of the time—he would elaborate in great detail on how he couldn't "do anything right."

In order to better understand how Freddy experienced the world, Dr. G. had him do some sensory processing and motor tasks. The results showed that Freddy was hypersensitive to both sound and touch, but was also under-reactive to movement and thus craved motion in space. So, while Freddy hated vacuum cleaner noises and rough, tight clothing and would startle if someone he had not seen touched him from behind, he would also jump or spin or pace about in order to create the sense of movement he craved.

The tasks also revealed important sensory and motor weaknesses that contrasted with Freddy's strong verbal memory and eye for detail. Physically, he found it hard to copy shapes, jump, or throw and catch a ball, and mentally he had trouble with visual-spatial problem solving. Freddy was unable to describe how to get to his school or to construct different types of patterns with blocks or drawings that involved going from one perspective to another. Thus, it was not surprising that Freddy would rather use his strong verbal skills to converse or bounce around to feed his craving for motion than sit still and write with a pencil or engage in a sport that required good motor skills.

When Dr. G. asked Freddy how he felt when he was overloaded by a noisy environment or people intruding on him, he described an unusual pattern. Instead of trying to avoid these sensations, as most hypersensitive children would have, Freddy described himself as becoming more active and "losing it." "I have to attack," he said. He seemed to need to combat what was overwhelming him rather than to calm himself down. When he became overloaded, he would become more active, aggressive, and agitated. By this point, despite his hypersensitivities, Freddy would begin seeking more sensation, not less, producing the very loud noises that he himself hated as well as eliciting loud noises and other unpleasant sensations from others. This would cause him to become even more overloaded, setting up a vicious circle of sensory overload and self-overloading behavior.

Watching Freddy's parents talk to and play with him, Dr. G. noticed that Ms. B. seemed to hang onto his every word, reacting anxiously and emotionally to whatever he said. Whenever Freddy would become upset, instead of calming and soothing him, Ms. B. began talking and moving faster, appearing anxious. Although she was obviously trying to help her son, Ms. B.'s approach merely upset Freddy more. Ms. B. explained that her own mother was anxious and often depressed. She remembered worrying a lot about her during her own childhood but being resentful as well, especially during adolescence.

Mr. B. interacted quite differently with Freddy. For him, dominance was the central issue: he appeared more concerned about who was in control and who listened to whom than anything else. Anytime Freddy failed to immediately follow his father's instructions or respond in a manner that Mr. B. considered appropriate, his father became visibly irritated. Mr. B.'s tone of voice betrayed seething, explosive anger which, although contained, was almost palpable in its intensity. When Freddy began getting agitated, Mr. B., rather than setting calm, persistent, firm limits, was drawn into power struggles with him.

Freddy's parents talked about their feelings of frustration, helplessness, and anger, as well as their worries about Freddy's future. Although they understood that a comprehensive approach was required to help their son, they couldn't help wishing for a miraculous, quicker solution.

After gathering all this information in early interview and observation sessions, Dr. G. summarized it and presented it to Freddy's parents in the form of a developmental profile, using the DIR model outlined earlier.

Freddy's Developmental Profile

Functional, Emotional, Developmental Capacities: Freddy's interview showed that he was able to stay focused in a calm, one-on-one situation, but quickly began "losing it" when his senses were overloaded. He engaged warmly and intensely with others, but became agitated and angry when they became too loud or too physically intrusive. Then Freddy's attitude suddenly cooled and trust turned to suspiciousness. Freddy could understand and use simple emotional gestures to communicate pleasure, warmth, assertiveness, and anger as well as more subtle feelings such as curiosity and competitiveness. However, with many feelings and in many circumstances he could do this only briefly. When Freddy was being soothed, particularly when he and his mother were calm together, he participated in the long chains of emotional communication that help a child learn to regulate intense negative feelings. But when conflicts or power struggles arose with his siblings, father or teachers, Freddy was unable to engage in such chains and became upset. He couldn't argue or exchange angry looks without completely losing it, as he himself admitted, nor could he express feelings of sadness, disappointment, or a sense of loss, even by using gestures. It was as if he had never experienced these feelings at all.

In using the DIR model, we try to understand how a child and caregiver communicate emotions before the child can use language or even symbols. Communication problems at this level often seem to underlie difficulties later expressed symbolically, sometimes through problem behaviors. Thus, much of the work that both therapists and parents need to do to help moody children needs to take place on a lower level of development, where communication is still pre-symbolic. Words are of limited value: gestures and symbols are also needed to help the child acknowledge and regulate more emotions. Once Freddy was able to deal more effectively with angry or agitated feelings, the assumption was that he would also be able to better regulate his behavior. In therapy and at home, Freddy would need to experience and express feelings of which he had heretofore been unaware, learn to label them with words, and explore how one feeling connected with another.

As we considered Freddy's symbolizing skills, we saw that he could be creative and imaginative, expressing a wide range of ideas. However, he could use symbols only with some feelings and ideas, failing to use them with others, especially feelings of loss, disappointment, and sadness, which he couldn't acknowledge. Freddy also had trouble symbolizing ideas that negotiated anger or competition. He could use words to describe anger or desire, but only to discharge these feelings, not to discuss them. For example, when he talked about arguing with his sister over which TV shows they would watch, Freddy would say, "She was in my way and I pushed her." He couldn't spontaneously say, "She was really getting me angry and I wanted to push her and change the channel to what I wanted to watch." Because Freddy couldn't talk about feelings, he acted them out, pushing his sister out of the way, for example. In contrast, he could talk about "enjoying" reading and talking with his mother and how he felt calm and warm.

In developing the DIR model, we have identified several different levels for the manner in which children or adults express feelings and wishes. Action or physical descriptions, such as Freddy's saying, "I pushed my sister" or "there's a storm in my tummy," are at the lowest level. Black-and-white global descriptions of feelings, such as "I hate everyone," are on an intermediate level. More specific, qualified descriptions involving cause and effect such as "I feel a little bit scared because today is my first day at my new school" are at a higher level.

Moving up through these levels helps a child learn to build bridges between ideas. Freddy's symbolizing skills showed a disparity in this respect, depending on what particular feeling was involved. While he could discuss loving feelings at the highest level—saying, for example, "I love my mother best when she takes me to the arcades," he could express emotions of anger/competition as well as loss/disappointment only at the lowest level. He couldn't reason logically or causally about these feelings, but instead locked onto fixed, polarized beliefs and acted them out: "They were trying to get me. I got them first."

At even higher levels involving attention to emotional subtleties—shades of gray rather than blacks and whites—Freddy's abilities were likewise selective. He could reflect somewhat subtly on dependent and loving feelings, but not at all on anger, competition, power struggles, loss, or disappointment. When these feelings surfaced, Freddy's thoughts tended to polarize and he acted them out.

Motor and Sensory Processing Profile: Contributing to Freddy's mood troubles were both biological and environmental patterns. On the biological side, he was hypersensitive to both sound and touch, while under sensitive to and thus craving movement in space. Freddy also had stronger auditory processing and verbal abilities and weaker visual-spatial processing and motor planning and sequencing capacities. These patterns, along with his interaction patterns with his parents, siblings, and teachers, contributed to his tendency to become easily overloaded. Freddy's hypersensitivity was not balanced by strengths that would have helped him cope with the overload by mentally organizing the input. Instead, Freddy's craving for movement caused him to seek sensory input when he became overloaded, creating even more sensory overload and eliciting overloading responses from others. This sensory processing profile made it difficult for Freddy to soothe himself, especially when he experienced feelings of anger or competition.

Environmental-family patterns: On the environmental side, neither of Freddy's parents was able to help him soothe himself and reflect on his feelings. Instead, both parents challenged him, though in different ways. His father directly overloaded him with his own seething anger, viewing Freddy primarily as a rival, much as he had experienced his own four siblings. Often he saw Freddy as angry when Freddy was, in fact, merely frightened. Freddy's mother's behavior, which he experienced as more caring and loving, did not overload Freddy as much as his father's did, but it tended to undermine Freddy's learning how to self-soothe. Ms. B. often saw Freddy as helpless and needy even when he was operating in a competent manner. By over-reacting to his upset feelings, she would make him even more upset. One can imagine what it must have been like for her to deal with Freddy as an exceptionally moody infant or toddler.

Her own anxious tendencies probably made it difficult for her, despite good intentions, to provide the extra comforting a child like Freddy needed.

At school, teachers and peers also tended to behave in ways that overloaded Freddy rather than soothing him. A number of Freddy's teachers were similar to Ms. B. in hovering anxiously over him. One particularly calming teacher, on the other hand, had a positive effect on Freddy: he had the least number of upsets when he was in her class. Freddy did best with peers who were passive and allowed him to dominate them and worst with peers who were competitive and controlling, as one might expect.

Freddy's Treatment Program

Freddy's developmental profile summarizes various aspects of his case: his emotional developmental levels, his biologically based sensory and motor characteristics, and his family, school, and peer experiences. Freddy, as previously stated, typifies the child with a bipolar mood pattern. Now that we understand the pattern, we must next consider how best to help a child like Freddy. Neither parents nor therapists can hope to do this alone. Children with rollercoaster moods need more than just good parenting or good therapy: they require a comprehensive, individualized treatment approach involving not only parents and therapists, but also psychiatrists, teachers, educational specialists, and other helping professionals.

Freddy's treatment program had several components, including individual psychotherapy with Freddy two times per week, work with Freddy's parents once a week, and work with Freddy's school to help teachers understand his challenges and design an individualized educational program to meet his needs.

The main goal of Freddy's psychotherapy was to help him progress to higher levels of emotional development. More specifically, Freddy needed help engaging in longer chains of emotional communication, in which he and Dr. G. worked together to regulate and fine-tune his mood. If Freddy became agitated and began bouncing around the room, for example, Dr. G. would deliberately talk to him in a soothing, comforting tone so as to quiet his mood. When Freddy became more apathetic and withdrawn, on the other hand, Dr. G. would try to brighten Freddy's mood by talking faster and using more animated gestures and facial expressions. If Freddy turned and walked away, Dr. G. would try to maintain the rhythm by getting up and walking too or by continuing the vocalizations. Dr. G.'s tone was soothing and followed Freddy's lead. Meanwhile, along with working with Freddy at the preverbal level in this way, Dr. G. would also try to help Freddy symbolize and talk about his feelings. Thus, he would work with him simultaneously at both the presymbolic and the symbolic levels of communication. This was appropriate because Freddy's challenges were at both levels.

Over a period of six months, Freddy made progress on both levels of emotional communication. He gradually responded to Dr. G.'s soothing tone of voice and interactive rhythm by becoming calmer. When talking about his father being unfair or the kids at school picking on him, he was able to remain quiet and controlled. He also began verbalizing negative feelings, shifting from descriptions of actions or bodily sensations to reflecting more directly on his emotions. Instead of talking about his "exploding insides" or how he was going to "punch" so-and-so, he might talk about "feeling like my insides were shouting . . . like I was *so* mad."

Once Freddy was able to symbolize and talk about feelings, he became able to use them as signals, so as to anticipate next steps. If he became aware of feeling angry, for example, he could then consider alternative actions: when his brother came into his room uninvited, he could think about going to his parents rather than having a tantrum. Freddy was able to do this because he had first become able to engage in soothing interchanges with Dr. G. and thus his feelings were now less overwhelming. He could become upset without feeling that his world was flying to pieces. Since his feelings were less intense, he was better able to symbolize them, talk about them, and use them as signals to which he could choose his response.

As Freddy's therapy progressed in this way, Dr. G. was able to help him explore some of the emotions that he had avoided, such as feelings of disappointment, loss, humiliation, and anger. Freddy's avoidance of these feelings was partly due to anxiety and not wanting to feel helpless. The problem was intensified by the fact that Freddy's family provides few opportunities to elaborate these feelings. Mr. B.'s confrontational approach only created extreme rage and fear in his son. Ms. B., on the other hand, anxiously hovered and overreacted to Freddy's demands. Within the family, feelings of disappointment and loss were rarely tolerated, experienced, or discussed in detail.

Dr. G., understanding this, was especially alert to situations during sessions in which Freddy might experience feelings of loss and disappointment, such as when Dr. G. needed to end the session and Freddy still had a lot to say or when Freddy was losing a game. At such times, Dr. G. asked how Freddy felt and explored the different levels of feelings involved. Freddy usually started off such discussions with descriptions of action: "I don't want to stop. I should be the one to decide." As his therapy continued, however, Freddy was able to describe another level of feeling by saying, for example, "I feel like you're punching me in the stomach." As Dr. G. helped Freddy to describe more subtle feeling states, Freddy began using words like "feeling empty," "hollow," and "all alone." Gradually, he was able to describe and be more aware of feelings in the category of loss and disappointment. He also came to see that he often felt humiliated when he experienced such feelings.

Dr. G. also helped Freddy become more aware of his various processing differences. Freddy knew he was gifted verbally—"I can argue so well"—but he was less aware of his weaknesses in motor planning, sequencing and visual-spatial thinking, as well as his hypersensitivity to sound and touch. He was also unaware of his tendency to seek out more sensation rather than become cautious and self-soothing when he felt overloaded. To help Freddy understand these biological aspects of himself, Dr. G. watched for opportunities when Freddy was describing a relevant situation or experience. If Freddy talked about "losing it" at a noisy school sporting event, Dr. G. talked with him about how he experienced different sounds and also different types of touch, such as a slap on the back or a hand on the shoulder. Over a period of months, Freddy came to see that both loud and low-pitched motorized sounds tended to overload him. He was able to identify a pattern in which, when overloaded, he sought out more of those sensations rather than finding a quiet place to self-soothe. Understanding this pattern helped Freddy begin to anticipate and interrupt his tendency to further overload himself and instead to calm himself down.

Freddy learned that mentally picturing events and anticipating feelings in advance was not something he did naturally and that "thinking with pictures is hard." He was used to using words rather than visual images. Therapy, therefore, also focused on anticipating tomorrow, especially concerning challenging situations, and anticipating feelings, routine reactions, and alternatives. Over time, Freddy strengthened his ability to visualize and anticipate.

Freddy's challenges in motor planning and sequencing were more difficult to work with. His therapist's first step was to help him appreciate how hard it was for him to carry out actions that involved many steps. Long division problems and long essays with many subpoints were frustrating for him. Simply helping him understand that these types of challenges were frustrating because of the way his physical equipment worked—in comparison to creative verbal expression, which was easy for him—helped Freddy to identify and describe some of the feelings associated with the frustration. He started out by just saying "I'm bad at stuff" or "My brain doesn't work." Over time, he experienced and voiced feelings bordering on disappointment: "I feel bad . . . low . . . when I'm lousy at stuff." Eventually, Freddy was able to accept that certain types of activities were especially hard for him, and allow himself to feel sad. He came to accept that these activities would require more patience and concentration than others.

Freddy also worked to change his perceptions in relationships with family, peers, and teachers. This part of his therapeutic work occurred over many years as he learned to describe, symbolize, and reflect on his own feelings and to recognize relationship patterns. He began to realize that he tended to get involved in two types of relationship patterns. One was competitive and confrontational, which he came to associate with his father. The other was more helpless, needy, and dependent in a demanding way, as was the case with his mother. Freddy came to see how both patterns only intensified his mood extremes. Both in the family and with peers and teachers, Freddy was gradually able to develop his relationship skills.

As Freddy became better able to represent experience, he communicated more clearly about current conflicts with statements such as, "My father is like a raging crazy bear, and I can make him go ape." He admitted that he took pleasure in seeing his father "lose it." He also revealed that while sometimes it scared him when his parents fought over him—Ms. B. felt that Mr. B. was too angry with Freddy—he liked "to see Mom get him." Over time, as Freddy became more aware of these feelings, he could accept his father's more frequent invitations to do activities together such as sports, which Mr. B. enjoyed.

Freddy's treatment program also included work with his parents. Mr. and Ms. B. participated in weekly meetings with Dr. G., who helped them to work towards the same goals at home that Dr. G. worked towards in his individual sessions with Freddy. The couple learned how to engage Freddy in long, playful or problem solving interactions during which parent and child worked together to co-regulate Freddy's negative feelings. Each parent also explored the roots of his or her own tendencies and misperceptions—Mr. B. seeing Freddy as a threatening rival and Ms. B. seeing him as completely helpless—and they moved toward a more soothing pattern that would help their son become more calm, confident, and assertive. In addition, Freddy and his father practiced motor planning and sequencing through sports activities that helped him get more control over his physical movements. They competed in such invented games as running fast, then at medium speed, then slowly and super slowly. Similarly, they practiced drumming, singing, dancing, and throwing balls.

Collaboration with Freddy's teachers helped them to foster the same patterns as with his parents. Dr. G. suggested ways for them to calm Freddy down in the classroom so he could experience a positive learning relationship. When Freddy was provocative or defiant, instead of taking him literally, the teacher simply helped him to calm down and verbalize and thus work his way out of an upset state. The school program also provided one-on-one tutoring for Freddy, based on a curriculum we had developed to foster motor planning and visual-spatial thinking.

Over a period of four years, Freddy has made considerable progress. He now evidences better mood regulation, he can experience disappointment and sadness—new feelings for him—and he no longer feels hopeless or depressed. Instead of seeing the world as unfair, he analyzes how he and others contribute to a problem. Recently, he had a long talk with his sister about a "fair plan" to borrow each others' CDs. He is able to express and reflect on a wide range of age-appropriate feelings, observing "shades of gray" in them. In addition, he can now compare how he feels to internalized standards and can admit, "Sometimes I get a little madder than I should, but I can talk myself down." While he remains hypersensitive to certain sounds and light touch, he can calm himself down in their presence and, rather than "upping the stakes," create a soothing environment for himself.

When he has lots of homework, is rejected by a peer (he now has a group of close friends), or gets into a power struggle with his father, Freddy can still become intense and argue his point longer than his parents would like him to. He can also look sad and talk about how "unfair" his parents are. But now, after a brief time of feeling agitated or sad, Freddy can step back and reflect on his feelings and even inject some humor into the situation. His behavior is far less impulsive, and his agitated or depressed spells are much briefer. Now that Freddy has acquired some new skills, his schoolwork, his friendships, and his family relationships are becoming age-appropriate, and he remains free of symptoms.

Summary and Discussion

In this chapter we presented a model for understanding and helping children with bipolar mood patterns. We illustrated this model by describing, in detail, the case of Freddy B., a nine-year-old boy. This model, which has its roots in our more general DIR model, doesn't focus on just one aspect of the pattern, but takes all three aspects: developmental stages, individual biologically based differences, and relationships patterns into account. The case of Freddy shows how these three aspects are interrelated and how therapists as well as parents, teachers, and other professionals need to constantly be aware of all of them.

In talking about Freddy, we observed that he was hypersensitive to sound and touch but under-sensitive to, and therefore craving, movement in space. When he became overloaded, instead of avoiding sensations, as most hypersensitive children do, he tended to seek more intense sensation, which led to a vicious circle in which he both over-loaded himself and elicited over-stimulating reactions from parents and teachers, which caused him to feel even more overloaded. In working with many moody children over the years, we have seen this pattern again and again.

In discussing Freddy's case, we noted that his extreme moods related partly to problems that occurred long before he could speak about or even symbolize his feelings, at the point when caregiver and child need to engage in long chains of interactions that co-regulate the child's mood. We observed that because of these problems Freddy had not developed the ability to fully symbolize or discuss his feelings and wishes. Especially with disappointment/sadness/loss and anger/competition, all he could do was discharge his emotions by acting them out. When he did talk about feelings, he tended to describe them only in terms of action or bodily sensations—"I pushed her out of my room!"—rather than in more abstract, differentiated terms— "I felt mad." Dr. G. helped Freddy to talk about his feelings on a higher level and to understand how his feelings were interrelated. He also helped him to progress from "black-and-white" to "gray-area" thinking. In addition, he helped Freddy's parents create experiences at home, and his teachers at school, that were geared to his specific developmental and biological challenges so as to better help him overcome them.

CHAPTER 2

A Closer Look at the DIR Model and Children with Mood Swings, including Bipolar Patterns

In Chapter 1, we introduced the Developmental, Individual-Difference, Relationship-Based (DIR) model, a useful tool for understanding many kinds of problems children have, including patterns of extreme moodiness. In this chapter, we'll look more closely at the DIR model and show how this model can give us a fuller understanding of mood swings in children than is provided by the mere list of symptoms typically used to diagnose bipolar disorder.

The Three Components of the DIR Model

According to the DIR approach, three dynamically related influences work together to direct a child's development. The first influence is the biological and genetic structures of the child's brain and body. These structures do not directly determine a child's behavior, but influence the ways in which a child is able to interact in his relationships with others. For example, if a child's brain has difficulty processing visual-spatial cues (what he sees), the child may have trouble reading facial expressions and gestures, which makes emotional communication more difficult and has a serious negative effect on the child's relationships. Likewise, if a child has trouble with motor planning and sequencing, he may not be able to make the gestures needed to communicate messages to others. The second influence on the child's development is his cultural and family environment. These factors affect not only the child, but also the child's caregivers and their interactions with the child. The third influence is the patterns of interaction between child and caregiver. The child brings his biological differences into these interactions and the care-

35

giver brings his or her family-cultural patterns and personal history into them. These three factors constantly interact to determine how successful the child will be at mastering key tasks of emotional development such as maintaining a calm mood, relating to others, and communicating emotions.

Functional, emotional developmental level. The child's functional emotional developmental level relates to the child's ability to pull together all of her capacities (motor, cognitive, language, spatial, and sensory) in order to achieve emotionally meaningful goals. These capacities include the ability to do the following:

- Attend to multisensory and emotional experiences—e.g., looking at, listening to, or following the movements of a caregiver—while maintaining a calm, regulated mood.

- Experience pleasure with caregivers and show a preference for certain caregivers through joyful smiles and gestures of affection.

- Initiate and respond to two-way presymbolic emotional communication, smiling back and forth with the caregiver, for example, or making cooing sounds.

- Organize long chains of cooperative emotional signals and social problem solving communications in which many *circles of communications* (back-and-forth messages) are opened and closed; be able to maintain communication across space, not just when the caregiver is right next to the child; and begin to develop a sense of having a "me" that exists within relationships.

- Use ideas as a basis for creative or imaginative thinking, giving meaning to symbols through pretend play or using words to meet needs, such as "Juice!"

- Build bridges between ideas as a basis for logic, reality testing, thinking, and judgment, e.g., engaging in arguments, conversations about opinions, or elaborate make believe dramas.

Individual differences in sensory/modulation, processing, and motor planning. These individual differences are biologically based. Some are the result of genetics, while others may relate to what happens before or immediately after birth, or as the child matures. They include the following:

- Sensory modulation, including hypo-and hypersensitivity to touch, sound, smell, vision, and movement in space.

- Sensory processing in each sensory modality: the ways in which the brain makes sense out of language and other sounds, sights, smells, and other incoming stimuli. Processing involves what the brain *does* with incoming sensations from the eyes, ears, nose, etc., which includes registering, decoding, and comprehending sequences and abstract patterns.

- Sensory-affective processing in each modality: the ability to make sense of and react to emotional signals, including translating intentions into actions—getting an idea and then doing it—such as picking up a ball or shouting "Give me the ball!"

- Motor planning and sequencing: the ability to do things "one after another," including the capacity to sequence actions, behaviors, symbols, thoughts, words, visual images, and spatial concepts.

Relationship and emotional interaction patterns. These include differences in caregiver, parent, family, and cultural patterns. The way in which the child interacts with her caregivers, family, and culture affects how her biology is shaped within the developmental progression and what capacities the child develops. Developmentally appropriate interactions with intimates mobilize the child's intentions and enable the child to broaden her horizons at each level of development and move from one functional developmental level to the next. In contrast, interactions which don't take the child's functional developmental level or individual differences into account may undermine progress. When caregivers, for example, expect a child to tie her shoes before she has the necessary motor planning skills in place, both parties become frustrated, the relationship suffers, and the child loses ground developmentally.

By taking all three components—functional emotional developmental level, differences in sensory processing, and interaction patterns with caregivers—simultaneously into account rather than over-focusing on just one aspect, the DIR model provides a framework for fully understanding a child's symptoms and behaviors. Such a comprehensive view enables us to more effectively identify risk patterns early on, as well as to develop comprehensive approaches to assessment, prevention, and treatment.

Within this framework, each major mental illness (depression, ADHD, autism, etc.), as well as various ways of being mentally healthy, appears to be characterized by a unique structure of interrelated developmental factors, sensory differences, and interaction patterns. Extremely moody children tend to display a common set of underlying regulatory problems and a common developmental profile. While each child with mood problems is different, the child with the bipolar pattern has a special signature that is quite specific. This common signature helps us distinguish this pattern from its close cousins, known as *comorbid* conditions.

Unique to children with severe mood swings are a set of cumulative developmental challenges that include biological factors that affect their ability to regulate feelings and thus their overall patterns of development. For example, if a child is born with a high activity level and high sensory reactivity, that child may be more prone to explosiveness, which in turn negatively affects family and peer relationships. Such cascades of events may put a child at risk for developing rollercoaster mood patterns. However, an appropriate early intervention program may, in many cases, be able to interrupt and restructure potentially bipolar developmental sequences.

A key element of a bipolar pattern lies in the child's response to his own sensations and emotions. Children with extreme mood cycles are unusually hypersensitive, easily overloaded by sensory information and extremely tuned into their environments. However, while the classic hypersensitive child shuts down and becomes shy and cautious when overloaded—hiding in a corner of the room, for example—children with bipolar patterns behave differently. These children, in addition to being hypersensitive to touch or sound, also tend to crave sensations. Thus, they often go into "active mode" when overloaded. Instead of becoming self-protective and cautious in response to over-stimulation, they become anxious and respond to their anxiety by going in the opposite direction: craving and seeking sensory experiences, often including movement in space. As they become more active, craving sensations, they overload themselves more, thereby escalating the challenge rather than solving it. They may become more and more agitated and/or aggressive, and caregivers, upset by such behavior, may intensify it by reacting emotionally and further overloading the child.

For example, Willie's mother takes him with her to the mall to do some shopping. Willie behaves appropriately in the car, but as soon as they're in the mall, he begins to run around, climbs up on the wall next to the fountain, and threatens to jump in. Willie's mother, understandably upset, starts screaming at Willie to come down from the wall. Further agitated, Willie jumps into the fountain and is subsequently hauled out by a security guard, who orders Willie's mother to take him home. This sequence of events arises from Willie's response to sensory input. Not only is Willie hypersensitive to sensations, he responds to overload by creating even more sensations that cause him to feel even more overloaded. A classically hypersensitive child, overloaded by the sensations of people walking back and forth, colorful objects being sold everywhere, flowing fountains, and all sorts of intense stimuli that a mall produces, might respond by closing his eyes, withdrawing to a corner, or focusing in on a single object in order to reduce the amount of input. Willie, however, responds by becoming wilder and wilder, and his mother's screaming only overloads him further. While she may feel that yelling at him will scare him out of misbehaving, such an approach does not work with children like Willie. Instead, what Willie needs, when he begins misbehaving, is for his mother to take him into the bathroom, where sensations are minimal, sit quietly with him and speak to him soothingly rather than angrily until he's able to calm himself.

Excessively moody children are typically hypersensitive to either sound or touch, usually to one more than the other, sound being the more common hypersensitive mode of the two (touch can be variable, and some children have a low pain threshold). The child's craving for movement in space often relates to undersensitivity in relation to vestibular (sense of movement) functioning. Thus, children with bipolar patterns combine elements of both the classic hypersensitive child and the classic sensation seeker.

As they become overloaded, these children become sensory-craving and active not only behaviorally but also in terms of a "rush of ideas." At such times, thoughts fly through their heads at lightning speed. When they're not overloaded by their physical or emotional world, on the other hand, they can be calm and easy-going. This differentiates them from the typical child with a hyperactive-impulsive ADHD pattern, whose motor activity level may run high most of the time.

The bipolar pattern occurs on two levels: physiological and psychological. At the physiological level, it's simply how the child's body works. If a child becomes overloaded due to hypersensitivity, sensation-seeking does not constitute a defense against psychological conflicts, but rather an automatic physiological reaction. When the senses become overloaded, the physiology simply shifts to the craving mode instead of to the shut-down mode, which is comparable to going into the fight mode rather than the flight mode in the case of the flight-fight reaction. A child is either born with such tendencies or acquires them during maturation due to exposure to toxic substances, traumatic stress, or other biologically destructive factors.

As a child becomes older, however, the pattern of hypersensitivity combined with sensory-craving acquires psychological meaning. At this point, the psychological level must also be addressed. From this standpoint, hypersensitive children can be divided into two categories: truly hypersensitive and sensory-craving/hypersensitive. The truly hypersensitive child, when overloaded, responds to anxiety by going into an avoidant mode, which can lead to phobic defenses. The child who is hypersensitive to movement in space, for example, becomes overcautious, refusing to climb to high places and jumps, and may become anxious and scared. In this way, the particular psychological defense is selected by the child's physiology.

On the other hand, the type of child who, when overloaded, responds to anxiety by shifting into the sensory-craving, active mode at a psychological level may develop counter-phobic defenses, going toward rather than away from what overwhelms or scares him. In each case, the child's physiology selects a different defense. Once the physiologically determined pattern becomes established, the psychological elements can take on a life of their own.

In addition, family and other environmental factors can compound the pattern because of its psychological meaning. If a hypersensitive/sensory-craving child is surrounded by anger and conflict, he may feel that it's dangerous to be vulnerable. Instead he assumes that he's omnipotent and invulnerable and becomes more and more counter-phobic, taking extreme risks and challenging authority. Soon the pattern becomes established. Now suppose that instead of being surrounded by negative intensity, the same child grows up in an environment where it's safe to be vulnerable and where, as soon as the child becomes overloaded and thus begins risk-taking, care-givers respond in a soothing manner, "Calm down, Sweetheart. You don't need to be so strong. It's OK to be scared sometimes. I know that noise bothers you." A child who grows up in such an environment may eventually learn to calm himself. While the environment is only one element of this bio-psychosocial challenge, in many situations it can either intensify or soften the challenge.

For adults to become engaged in power struggles with hypersensitive/sensory-craving children is entirely normal. This often happens because adults do not understand why these children misbehave and believe that the methods that work with other kinds of children work with them. Once they understand how to deal with the child differently, they can begin to head off problems before they become extreme. The secret of success is to learn to recognize what's happening when your child's agitation is just getting started, at level 1 or 2 (the lowest levels on the intensity scale) and thus intercede before it escalates to level 8 (the highest level). This is not always easy; with some children, agitation can build up from 1 to 8 with lightning speed. At level 2 or 3, an adult can intercede on the child's behalf and help her to calm down, saying, "I know that noise is scary and we're going to tell that noise to go away. Let's do it together." At higher levels of agitation, this does not work.

For example, one boy, Jason, became rapidly more agitated when overloaded and began hitting. Dr. G., his therapist, worked with his parents on letting Jason "be the boss" where his own sensory input was concerned. As the boss, he could order the noise to stop or order his parents to stop before he became overloaded. Jason could also tell his parents when his sisters were upsetting him. Prior to this, Jason was aware that when there was too much noise he got wild, but he failed to recognize that he could decide how he would react. Dealing with a child this way requires more than mere logic. It is not simply a matter of talking to the child, as parents often believe; they must engage with him at a deep level of the relationship so that he feels that they are working with him to protect him.

Once a child escalates past level 4, nothing anyone says is going to be right, no matter how logical it might be. To reason with a child at all, one must intervene before the level of agitation passes level 4. Beyond this level, the best strategy is to let the storm run its course, keep the child safe, and try to find a calming rhythm that works for that child. Each child may require a slightly different approach, but the key is to try to intervene before agitation escalates to level 4.

Many children with bipolar patterns vacillate between agitation and anger and blaming others. They can also be extremely self-critical and self-blaming, saying, "I can't do anything right." "It's all my fault." "Everyone would be better off if I wasn't here!" This is the other half of the pattern. It reveals a tendency towards polarized, all-or-nothing thinking: it's either "all your fault" or "all my fault." The goal is to help the child advance beyond polarized thinking and coping to more differentiated "grey area" ways of dealing with feelings, to be able to say, for example, "I'm a little sad and a little mad."

When children with this pattern are helped to calm themselves and progress to "grey area" patterns of dealing with feelings, they are less likely to be counter-phobic and aggressive, so risk-taking and self-blame are often less extreme. Thus, if the child can learn to verbalize and feel comfortable with vulnerability, she may still become agitated or sad, but over time she may develop the ability to observe herself as well as to regulate her feelings more effectively.

In auditory processing and language, extra-moody children fit two different patterns. One type, relatively free of other problems, has relative strengths in auditory processing and language skills, achieving higher scores for verbal skills than performance skills on neuropsychological tests. The other type displays more diverse developmental challenges, with language and auditory processing as well as motor planning problems. Along with their bipolar symptoms, they may have multiple learning problems and other difficulties.

Often the children who are relatively stronger in auditory processing and language tend to be overly attentive to details, focusing on the "trees" rather than the whole "forest." They are sensitive and alert and may have strong memory and recognition skills, but they have relative weaknesses in big picture thinking—the ability to recognize the forest—and may have some difficulties in motor planning and sequencing. Most psychological test batteries focus more on visual memory and recognition of individual trees rather than on forest recognition. Thus, psychologists may fail to identify weaknesses in this area in children with mood swings, including bipolar patterns.

The children who have developmental challenges across the board along with their bipolar symptoms often tend to use magical thinking, believing they can will the rain into stopping when they want to play baseball, for example, and may have a distorted sense of reality due to their multiple developmental challenges. Some have significant difficulties in the basics of relating and communicating. They require the same assessment, diagnostic, and treatment strategies as the first group, but they also need help with their additional developmental problems, e.g., a comprehensive approach, often including an intensive home program, speech and language therapy, occupational therapy, special educational approaches, psychotherapy, and family guidance.

Extremely moody children tend to elicit punitive and/or inconsistent rather than empathic, consistent responses even from skilled, loving caregivers. Because these children vacillate between becoming depressed and becoming aggressive and energized, it's also easy for parents to allow them to become symbiotic, so that the parent loses his or her sense of individuality and instead becomes enslaved to the child's every whim and over-protects her from those who try to facilitate their separation. Often parents vacillate between over-protectiveness and rigid punitiveness with children who have these challenges, which creates a highly unstable situation. Because the challenges tend to escalate as well as alternate, it's difficult to help such a child learn to regulate feelings and observe himself or herself rather than to act out.

The Developmental Profile

As a result of the biological and environmental factors we've described, children with bipolar patterns tend to display a common functional emotional developmental profile with some of the following characteristics, which are summarized in Table 1.

Regulation. Children with bipolar patterns tend to combine sensory hypersensitivities and extreme sensory-craving, thereby overloading themselves as they become anxious and overwhelmed. They also tend to have weaker motor planning and higher level visual-spatial than auditory processing except for those who have both challenges.

Engagement. Most children with extreme mood patterns tend to connect with others easily and many are very close to at least one parent. The relationship is characterized by engagement, warmth, and involvement. These children are generally not self-absorbed. Often they eagerly seek closeness and warmth with others. Some children with bipolar patterns, however, also evidence other developmental challenges, including difficulties with basic engagement and communication.

Purposeful gesturing. Most children with these patterns can be highly purposeful and deliberate in their gestures as well as extremely tuned into and reactive to their environment. They can create reciprocal interactions with others. Children with bipolar symptoms often, however, show weaknesses in two tasks at the level of emotional gesturing. They fail to engage in long, regulated chains of reciprocal gestural conversation, which are necessary for normal development; also, they're unable to sustain chains of reciprocal gestures with each specific emotion. In negotiating aggressive feelings, for example, they often lack the fine-tuned system that would enable them to engage in fifty circles of communication in which child and caregiver work together to soothe or otherwise regulate the child's emotions. Consequently, they may never develop the ability to regu-

Table 1:   The Developmental Profile of the Bipolar Child

Regulation	Tends to combine sensory hypersensitivities and extreme sensory-craving; weak motor planning and higher level visual-spatial than auditory processing, except when child has both.
Engagement	Tends to connect with others easily. Relationships characterized by warmth, engagement, and involvement.
Purposeful Gesturing	Can be highly purposeful and deliberate with gestures as well as extremely tuned into and reactive to the environment.
Preverbal Co-regulated Affective Problem solving Interactions	Major problems establishing long chains of reciprocal interactions; difficulties with self-soothing, controlling behavior, engaging fully in social interactions, and problem solving.
Representational (Symbolic) Level	Can be highly creative and have rich dramatic play. Themes are inconsistent and child may have trouble acting out some specific feelings while having no difficulty with others.
Logical Thinking (building bridges between ideas)	Stays polarized in "all-or-nothing thinking." Difficulty with gray-area thinking in connection with aggression, loss, and vulnerability.

late aggressive impulses at the level of gestural communication. Instead of simply shaking a fist, they'll go ahead and hit someone. They're often better at being flirtatious, warm or loving (especially when they're not angry or overloaded). Their emotional expressiveness tends to be less differentiated from their thinking—so that they act out feelings instead of talking about or otherwise processing them—with those emotions over which they have the least control. They may have stronger emotions around certain themes and some emotions may be slightly more differentiated than others.

Preverbal co-regulated affective problem solving interactions. Children with bipolar patterns typically experience major problems at the preverbal level—the level immediately before they begin to develop spoken language—around establishing long chains of reciprocal emotional interactions; thus, they have difficulty soothing themselves, controlling their own behavior, and engaging fully in social interactions and problem solving. This pattern, which begins in the phase of purposeful gesturing, continues into this phase and beyond.

The reciprocal emotional gesturing system is extremely important. When it's not well developed, the child both misreads the gestures of others and makes inappropriate gestures herself. A child may become aggressive because she's unable to decode the signals and see what's coming and she's taken by surprise. She then feels the intensity of her rage going rapidly from 0 to 8 and is not able to warn the other person, "Hey, I'm about to have a tantrum."

As children continue to develop during the second year of life, complex co-regulated emotional signaling between child and caregiver enables most toddlers to learn to regulate their own moods and behaviors and thus tame catastrophic emotions such as fear and rage. When a child is capable of rapid back-and-forth interactions with her caregiver, she is able to negotiate how she feels. If she's annoyed, she can make a look of annoyance or a sound or hand gesture. Her mother can respond with a gesture indicating, "I understand," "OK, I'll get the food more quickly," or "Can't you wait just one more minute?" Whatever the response is, if it's responsive to the child's signal, she's getting some immediate feedback that can modulate her response. The anger may be modulated by the notion that Mother's going to do something, even if she can't do it immediately. Just the sound of her voice signals to the child that she's getting that milk bottle ready and it's coming soon. If Mother can use a soothing voice and meet the child at her fast-paced, frantic rhythm of back-and-forth cueing and gradually slow her down through a calming rhythm—down-regulating her emotions to a lower level of intensity—all the better. We often do this intuitively in a close relationship when we're upset or angry. However, some of us get nervous, speed up and "up the stakes" by taking the other person's anger personally. We up-regulate the rhythm rather than slowing and calming. If a caregiver can slow and soothe the child via emotional gestures as well as words (the gestures, however, are far more powerful), the child learns better and better regulation.

Consider the following example. Tommy, a toddler, is pushing his bottle away with an angry glance at his mom. She puts her hand out to take it from him, uses soothing tones to convey empathy and, in a slower rhythm, offers her finger to make contact. Tommy squeezes it, feels a bit reassured, and looks expectantly as Mom holds up a finger food to see if he wants it. He waves his hand to convey "yes." Tommy knows that his anger is being responded to, and thus his mood has been down-regulated. Now suppose Tommy, instead of being angry, is looking a little sad, subdued, and self-absorbed. Mom energizes (up-regulates) and pulls him into a joyful interaction, and he learns to regulate in the other direction. Different feelings, from joy and happiness to sadness to anger to assertiveness can become a part of finely tuned and regulated emotional interactions in which subtle reciprocal patterns come into play rather than all-or-nothing ones.

Often, without the modulating influence of an emotional response, the child's feeling may simply become more intense. The child may end up overwhelmed by global, unadulterated feelings of anger, rage, or fear and respond with avoidance, withdrawal or self-absorption, as is characteristic of very young infants in the early months of life. For example, David was an intense twelve-month-old who liked to be on the move. When his gestures were not read and responded to and drawn into interactions, he quickly became agitated and butted his mom with his head or tried (sometimes successfully) to bite her.

When this system of co-regulated affective gesturing does not develop as indicated, we tend to see more agitation and aggression. Children who are over-sensitive, crave sensation, or have weak motor sequencing or visual-spatial processing can have a harder time developing this system. Children with bipolar patterns can have all or some of these regulatory challenges.

As they develop more ideas, some children with these challenges become excessively suspicious of other people's intentions, which overloads them even more. In cases where counter-phobic patterns develop, these can also intensify the problem. If caregivers are punitive rather than empathetic, regulating, and firm, the child can easily become more angry, depressed, suspicious, and/or anxious. Once he becomes angry and mistrustful, he can overload himself because he experiences his environment as hostile. Thus, it's easy for moody children to become trapped in all sorts of vicious circles.

Family members, educators, and clinicians need to create soothing environments for children and work to improve co-regulated emotional signaling. They can help children to develop the coping strategies they need to deal more effectively with their own biologically based processing challenges; to become better perceivers and initiators of emotional cues; and at the same time work on setting firmer, more consistent behavioral limits.

The more a given child is both hypersensitive and sensory-craving and the weaker the visual-spatial and motor planning systems, the more difficult it is for him to learn to communicate emotions through gestures. For example, if motor planning is compromised, a child may not have enough motor control to make recognizable gestures. If visual-spatial processing is weak, a child is not able to read another person's signals and gestures from across the room. A companion needs to be right next to the child and to use touch (known as proximal modes), rather than just visual and auditory (known as distal modes) exchanges for communication to take place. Negotiating in distal modes facilitates a more flexible style of exchange: one can flirt, wink, make sounds or use arm gestures from across the room. This is a much more subtle, flexible system than the proximal modes and is the way adults do most of their gesturing. Children who have to use the proximal modes due to poor visual-spatial and motor planning may often annoy others with in-your-face intrusiveness.

The reciprocal emotional gesturing system is what enables a person to go from catastrophic emotions that provoke global reactions such as avoidance, flight, or fight to symbolic communication. It is the mediating system between feelings and language. When he feels extremely angry, for example, the intensity of his anger may lead to him acting out his anger through some sort of extreme behavior such as yelling, smashing, or running away. The reciprocal emotional gesturing system, however, allows him to modulate his anger and, instead of acting it out, use his emotion as a signal that something is amiss. This is a prerequisite for symbol formation, thinking, and self-observation.

Thus, children with bipolar patterns need to develop a reciprocal emotional gesturing system to learn to cope with the vicissitudes of their own unique biology. Medications such as mood stabilizers can help calm a person and reduce over-reactivity, but only new learning can improve emotional signaling.

Representational or symbolic level. Many children with bipolar patterns are highly creative and have rich dramatic play. Their dramas, however, are not often equally effective in acting out all feelings. A child may, for example, be able to dramatize nurturing feelings with a pretend tea party, but be unable to use pretend play to organize aggression, acting it out instead. If children feel warm and affectionate and are not overloaded or agitated, they may dramatize their feelings skillfully, but if they become angry and agitated in the course of their play, instead of channeling feelings into elaborate subplots such as a complicated science fiction drama, they may regress into banging action figures around which, although still in the pretend mode, is not truly representational. All they're doing is blowing off steam, not communicating feelings. They use words, but their words merely describe events and accompany the discharge of emotions rather than representing feelings. True, they're hitting a substitute action figure instead of Daddy, but this is nonetheless an emotional discharge rather than communication. This is also the case when an adult yells without hitting, using words not for the purpose of representing a thought or a feeling, but to intimidate. In addition, when a child with bipolar patterns becomes more self-critical and depressed, he can shift to the opposite extreme, playing or talking about how "bad" he is as if it's a reality rather than a feeling.

Logical thinking or representational differentiation (building bridges between ideas) and higher level reflective thinking. This pattern continues as children move up the ladder into logical thinking, progressing through triangular thinking, multi-causal thinking, and relativistic (gray-area) thinking, and developing an internal sense of having a self and even a set of internal standards. At each of these higher stages of development, extra-moody children tend to remain more polarized in all-or-nothing patterns, particularly having difficulty with modulated, gray-area thinking in connection with feelings of aggression, loss, and vulnerability, feelings around which they were unable to engage in pretend play or long chains of co-regulated gesturing. Without appropriate treatment or favorable life experiences, these patterns may continue throughout childhood and adolescence and into adulthood.

As children with bipolar patterns move towards adulthood, they may have particular difficulty learning to deal with feelings of disappointment, loss or sadness. They often shift from feeling agitated or angry to global depression. Feelings of disappointment, loss or sadness require an awareness of subtle internal feeling states, which make them difficult for these children to process because of their tendency to perceive feelings as all-or-nothing—furious or terrified, for example, rather than *a little* angry or *a little* scared. Such inadequacies in gray-area thinking may be associated with the failure to develop an adequate emotional gesturing system.

In many cases, early preventive interventions may be able to interrupt the pattern we've been describing, which does not necessarily always lead to bipolar-type difficulties. Whether these tendencies develop into a full-fledged bipolar pattern may depend on the intensity of the child's biological tendencies, the child's environment, and the types of interventions used by professionals.

As children with bipolar patterns become older and life becomes more complicated, they may intensify their hypersensitive/sensory-craving pattern and respond to a variety of issues such as loss of relationships or anxieties about dating and sexuality by seeking further stimulation and counter-phobically doing whatever they find most frightening. Any challenge which triggers vulnerable feelings can lead such a child to further overload himself. Thus the child who is initially overloaded by sound or touch or intense emotions may later become overloaded by internal conflicts and a variety of feelings if his tendency to respond to anxiety with sensory-craving and activity is not changed.

As children mature, professionals who work with them need to differentiate bipolar patterns from patterns associated with other disorders. The pattern we're describing is different from the pattern that is typical for children with conduct disorders. The child with a conduct disorder is typically not hypersensitive to sound or touch. He tends to be sensory- and movement-craving, under-reactive to pain, and often a dare devil. Children with bipolar patterns and conduct disorders may look similar, but the underlying pathways associated with misbehavior are often different. The hypersensitive/sensory-craving child's misbehavior can be traced to anxiety and hypersensitivity to sensations, while the purely sensory-craving child misbehaves often because most of her senses *are* under-reactive.

Children with anxiety and depression, like those with bipolar patterns, are often hypersensitive to sensations. They become overloaded by sound and touch but, unlike children with bipolar characteristics, they tend to become cautious or inhibited in response to the overload. When overloaded, they do not evidence sensory-craving leading to aggression or agitation.

The oppositional child is also often hypersensitive to sensations. She is often, however, strong at big picture thinking. She tends to have stronger visual-spatial integrative (seeing the forest) capacities than the child with bipolar symptoms. What distinguishes the defiant or oppositional child from the hypersensitive, fearful child is her determination to control her world rather than to avoid or become overwhelmed by it. The oppositional child may be rigid, locked into certain patterns and intent on fending off overload, depression, or anxiety by controlling her world. She does not escalate and become sensory-craving in the same way the child with bipolar patterns does.

The child with Attention Deficit Disorder (predominantly inattentive ADHD) or Attention Deficit Hyperactivity Disorder (ADHD) may evidence many different regulatory patterns. Some children diagnosed with ADD are hypersensitive, which makes them overloaded and distractible. Other children with this diagnosis are undersensitive, self-absorbed with low muscle-tone, and also distractible, but for a different reason than the hypersensitive child. Some children with ADHD features are sensory-craving, but not exclusively when overloaded, as in the case of children with bipolar patterns. The regulatory characteristic we have found to be most often associated with ADHD is motor planning and sequencing problems. Thinking before acting and step-by-step planning is hard for them. Children with ADHD usually have more severe motor planning problems than children with bipolar disorder. The fact that ADHD and bipolar patterns share some underlying regulatory features may explain why they so often appear as comorbid.

A Comprehensive Program of Preventive Interventions

Children with bipolar patterns need professional interventions at several different levels. If treatment is begun early enough in the developmental pathway, the focus can be on prevention. If it's begun later on, interventions must be more comprehensive. The overall goals of treatment for these children are the following:

- To improve self-calming through soothing (most important).

- To deepen the pleasurable part of important relationships, especially where they've been polarized into power struggles and these struggles have begun to compromise trust. The child needs to feel again that he can trust and rely on the world. This increased trust eventually becomes the basis for dealing with vulnerability.

- To improve the regulation of emotions and mood by developing the reciprocal emotional regulatory gesturing system. By means of back-and-forth emotional gesturing, the child must learn to regulate emotions as well as to process sensory stimuli, internal sensations, and interactions that may overload or agitate her.

Consider an example of Dr. G. working preventively with Jody, a toddler who is hypersensitive to sound. Dr. G. works on three developmental levels at once to calm Jody down by using soothing tones, maintaining a pleasurable relationship while deepening his trust, and helping him to down-regulate when he becomes even slightly agitated. Dr. G. exchanges emotional signals while gradually increasing Jody's exposure to noise, starting at very low noise levels and very gradually turning up the volume. Dr. G. remains engaged in a compelling visual, vocal, and gestural contact with Jody while maintaining a soothing, calming rhythm. If he becomes a little frightened or starts to become even slightly agitated, Dr. G. increases his engagement and rhythmic communication with the child in order to help him stay calm. This is a little like "talking someone down." Dr. G. maintains emotional contact with Jody in the presence of stressors. His next step is to help Jody's parents learn to work with him in the same way.

For them, this is like doing a dance: Jody's mother learns to start at his overagitated level, then slow the dance down. If Jody is running around the room, she'll begin by running with him, but instead of letting the activity get out of control, she gradually shifts down to a slow motion game of running with the ball in order to down-regulate her son.

As children develop capacities for talking and thinking, we work on three additional goals:

- To foster the verbal or symbolic representation of the full range of emotions, including anger, loss, and agitation.

- To foster the integration of emotions in gray-area thinking rather than their polarization.

- To foster self-observation and reflection rather than action.

These goals are implemented, as are the first three goals, through a comprehensive home and therapy program. The work with parents and other family members at home is highly important and can be divided into four components: spontaneous Floortime, semi-structured play, anticipatory problem solving discussions, and physical play.

Working with children with bipolar patterns requires a particularly rigorous program of spontaneous Floortime at home, in which the caregiver allows the child to take the lead. Floortime gives parents the opportunity to work with the child on all her developmental levels at the same time, up to the highest level of which she is currently capable. During this time, parents help the child to broaden and regulate the full range of feelings and ideas appropriate for her developmental level. They also try to help the child work on a variety of new skills simultaneously: attending, relating, and purposefully interacting with emotional gestures in multiple circles of communication; engaging in a continuous flow of back-and-forth problem solving during co-regulated emotional interactions; and, if the child is ready, using words to elaborate a broad range of ideas and feelings creatively and logically. The key to success is following the child's natural interests and mobilizing spontaneous uses of communication. This means not only following the child's lead but also challenging the child to engage in longer and longer chains of co-regulated emotional interactions. How much Floortime a child needs varies from one child to another. Children with bipolar patterns typically need a minimum of four twenty-minute sessions of Floortime a day, two with each parent in a two-caregiver family. This is an essential component of the program.

Semi-structured activities should include two important activities: problem solving and anticipatory problem solving, including visualization. The model used for this is the "Six Steps to Problem Solving" as described in *Playground Politics* and *The Challenging Child* by Stanley Greenspan. Using these six steps, the child learns to anticipate challenges and visualize his feelings as well as possible solutions to problems. Caregivers need to do this with the child at least once every day. If a child is weak in visualization, he may need to do extra work on visualizing feelings.

In addition, parents need to engage their child in modulation games where the child runs (fast-slow-super slow) or plays a drum (loud-soft-super soft) one to four times per day. At least a couple of times per day, a child with motor planning problems needs to do a real physical workout involving sensory motor activities (throwing, catching, kicking) and visual-spatial problem solving, as in treasure hunts with younger children and more advanced exercises with older children such as are described in Furth and Wachs' *Thinking Goes to School.*

In our own work, we coach parents in two ways: first, by watching them play with their child and making suggestions; and second, by scheduling regular times during which parents can talk about their own feelings and discuss how best to help the child progress up the developmental ladder. If we're seeing the child twice a week individually, seeing the parents work with the child once a week, and seeing the parents once a week alone, that makes four meetings per week. Some parents cannot engage this many sessions; in such cases, we may see the child once a week and then see the parents with the child once a week, spending half the time watching the parent play with the child and the other half talking with them about family issues.

The home program, as we've described it, is essential to the child's progress. With boys especially, it's important that the father as well as the mother be involved. If a child is going to learn to deal with aggression, vulnerability, and humiliation and feel that it's safe to be vulnerable, he needs a close relationship with his father. The distant father is perceived as much more threatening than the warm, nurturing, present father.

With children who can verbalize or symbolize feelings, both the therapist and the parents need to help the child not only to interact reciprocally around anger, vulnerability, weakness, and sensory-craving, but also to symbolize or verbalize these feelings and related issues. We try to help the child deal with his emotions through talking and play. For example, we help the child, through a variety of play characters, to express a wide range of feelings, including fear, vulnerability, or humiliation, themes with which many children struggle. These themes need to be processed gradually, within a long-term therapy relationship. Once we see how the themes play out in therapy sessions, we then guide the parents in handling these emotions during their home Floortime. Thus, the therapy session not only helps the child to grow emotionally but also gives us the knowledge needed to advise the parents.

If the child is able to build bridges between ideas, we also work on reflective, big picture thinking. This involves labeling and elaborating on feelings, recognizing connections between emotions, and understanding how patterns work. For example, we might ask a child what it feels like when he becomes overloaded. "Nervous, like the world's coming to an end," he might answer. What does he do when he gets nervous? He "runs around and gets crazy." What does it feel like when you're crazy? "Well, I don't feel scared at least." This is traditional therapy, but with children with bipolar patterns we work with certain themes a bit more, particularly humiliation, fear, vulnerability, weakness, and anger, and also work at the earlier levels of engagement and co-regulated emotional gesturing.

As the child advances to the higher levels—triangular, multi-causal thinking, gray area or relativistic thinking, and eventually making judgments about his own feelings from a standpoint of an internalized "me"—we must help him to negotiate the transition into these stages.

The child's educational program needs to employ the principles outlined earlier in fostering calm, regulated interactions and the capacity to better symbolize and reflect on feelings and events. Implementing these principles requires that educators work closely with parents and therapists as a collaborative team. Therapists and teachers should confer frequently with parents, and communicate also with other professionals who may work with the child, such as speech therapists or occupational therapists.

Not all children with extreme moods have the same needs for additional services. Some may have specific learning challenges in the area of motor planning and sequencing; others have problems with high level visual-spatial "forest" thinking (in contrast with visual recognition or memory); and still others may have difficulties with language and/or aspects of cognitive functioning. Some have difficulties in all these areas. In fact, we have noted bipolar patterns in children with a variety of special needs. Extra moody children may also evidence strengths in some learning and academic areas.

Whatever unique developmental challenges a child may have, a comprehensive program should be organized to help her master them. This includes a thorough medical evaluation to rule out medical disorders that may be contributing to the child's behavioral challenges, (e.g., thyroid disorders) and possible treatments for them. Next, the therapist reviews the child's developmental history, including medical disorders, nutrition, patterns of growth and development, sleeping, eating, and attention patterns, relationship capacities, thinking, learning, and processing capacities, self-regulatory capacities, as well as the family history of these processes, including any family history of mental illness and compromises in optimal mental health.

In considering whether to prescribe medications for mood disorders, including bipolar patterns, it's important for professionals to view possible interventions within the context of the child's age and developmental level so as to decide whether they may be effective. It's also important to thoroughly explore the family patterns and the child's interactions with others as well as his own strengths and weaknesses. In many cases we have found it helpful to begin a comprehensive program which supports the child's capacity for regulating mood and behavior and for improving developmental, processing, and learning challenges, as well as working on emotional, social, and family functioning. This program should be in place for a reasonable period of time before we explore the issue of medication.

If and when medication is prescribed, we then monitor the child's functioning closely for both improvements in various areas as well as possible negative reactions such as increased reactivity, irritability, distractibility, aggression, fragmented or polarized thinking, signs of a tic disorder, obsessive-compulsive patterns, increased activity level, preoccupations, patterns of self absorption, and new problems interacting with peers at school or in the family. Not infrequently, when antidepressants are used with older children with bipolar mood patterns, we observe increased reactivity, irritability, and potential for aggression, as well as the potential for more fragmented or polarized thinking. We have also noticed diminished reflective thinking and engagement in age-appropriate relationships, school activities, and family patterns with the use of mood stabilizers. While many children may benefit from the use of medications, it's important to monitor their responses closely, especially because children often change rapidly in terms of their developmental capacities. What's helpful at one age or stage may not be so helpful at another.

Carla: A School-Age Girl
with a Bipolar Mood Pattern

Thus far, we have described childhood mood swings, including bipolar patterns, mainly in abstract terms, though giving examples along the way. In this chapter and the following chapter, we illustrate these ideas and provide a more comprehensive picture by presenting a detailed description of our work with two children, Carla and Jimmy. We hope this gives parents a deeper understanding of what extreme mood swings are all about and also helps professionals to work more effectively with children troubled by rollercoaster moods.

Case Background

Carla's mother, Ms. L., brought her in for a psychiatric evaluation with Dr. G. because she was worried about Carla's frequent rages, her chronic irritability, and her long periods of crying and depression. On many days, she was irritable and cranky from early in the morning to late at night. In the course of a typical day, Carla's mood would shift many times from euphoria to extreme despair. At one moment she would be on top of the world, singing happily or bragging that she could get the best grades in her class without doing any homework, and at the next she would become enraged or begin crying violently for no apparent reason. In addition, getting Carla to bed at night was an exhausting ordeal. Every night, Carla would protest that she wasn't tired and would use every possible strategy, complaining that she didn't have enough time to play, getting out of bed because she was still hungry, calling out to her mother because she had forgotten to tell her something, to delay going to sleep. Then, when she had finally settled down, she would wake up again and was often up and about during the night.

A single parent struggling to raise Carla alone, Carla's worried, frazzled mother could not figure her daughter out. Ms. L. had tried to remain calm and empathic when Carla was upset, but to no avail. When she tried to be firm and set clear limits, Carla would whine, cry, and throw tantrums, continuing on until Ms. L. became exhausted and gave in.

In school Carla was struggling both socially and academically. The other children chose not to play with her because she was bossy and would not share during play activities, and she had no friends at all. On the playground, she was usually off by herself. She would not try to play with other children, nor would she be invited by the others to do so.

Carla had no outstanding academic strengths, though she was stronger at decoding words while reading than in other areas. She could not, however, sit still long enough to read whole assignments. She could handle a pencil or crayon well and seemed to enjoy drawing and other art projects. Math was especially hard for her, as she had trouble learning and remembering basic addition and subtraction facts. Carla was not able to keep up with her work. She and her mother spent hours trying to finish up the piles of unfinished assignments that were a source of constant battles and allowed Carla and her mother almost no pleasurable time together.

Carla's early infancy had not been unusual. She was a happy baby who smiled, cooed, and babbled when adults played with her. Her mother recalled that she was active and seemed curious about her surroundings. At seven months, while looking out of a window, Carla pointed to a bird and repeated "Bir! Bir!" excitedly. But dramatic changes took place as she moved into toddlerhood. Her activity level and emotional intensity increased dramatically as she began to crawl and then to walk. When she wanted something, she would scream until she was finally given what she wanted. Her screaming tantrums were unrelenting; she could not be distracted. In addition, when she couldn't get what she wanted, she began to bang her head against hard surfaces, a behavior which continued through her seventh year. Carla was able neither to soothe herself nor to allow others to soothe her. Also, Carla seemed to develop hypersensitivities, as evidenced by her extreme startle response and habit of covering her ears when she encountered sudden and/or loud noises. Bright lights bothered her and she became cranky in brightly lit rooms. Sudden movements also seemed to upset her and make her irritable.

By the time Carla was four, she had changed from a happy infant to a sad, irritable, whiny child. She threw tantrums constantly, she had developed no self-control at all, and her mood was usually negative and extremely irritable.

A year before she was referred for treatment, when Carla was seven, she saw a psychiatrist, who placed her on Tofranil, a tricyclic antidepressant, which led to even more irritability, agitation, and tantrums. This was then followed by trials of two different selective serotonin reuptake inhibitors (SSRIs), first Prozac and then Paxil. These medications made her both more hyperactive and more emotionally overreactive while doing nothing to help her irritability, sleeplessness, or tantrums. For her sleep problem, she was placed on another medication, Clonidine, which made her "spacey." Finally, just prior to seeing Dr. G., Carla was placed on a mood stabilizer, Depakote, which did seem to help somewhat. Her behavior improved, and she seemed less irritable and depressed. She was also able to pay attention for longer periods of time and was willing to accept help with her homework.

Carla's parents were divorced when Carla was an infant and her father had not seen her since her early infancy. As Carla's mother had to work fulltime and there were no family members in the immediate geographic area, Carla was placed in fulltime daycare as a toddler. On the surface she seemed to make a good adjustment; no unusual behaviors or learning problems were reported. The environment was play-based and few demands were placed on Carla while she was there. She was basically free to do what she wanted. However, this environment did not give her enough opportunities to learn to regulate her emotions interactively, which requires lots of back-and-forth gestures and words with comforting, empathic caregivers.

Carla's mother, a neatly dressed and groomed woman in her mid-thirties, was a successful financial analyst, in good health, and, except for dealing with Carla's difficulties, managing well. Carla was her only child.

Carla's family history contained mood disorders on both sides. Carla's maternal uncle suffered from major depression and probable manic depression. Her maternal grandmother had an unspecified severe mental illness, and her maternal grandfather had an affective disorder. In addition, hyperactive behaviors were reported on Carla's father's side.

Carla's Evaluation

When Dr. G. first met Carla in his waiting room, she was crouched down against the side of her chair next to her mother, head balanced on her fisted hands, face set in an angry scowl. As Dr. G. greeted Carla, she grunted, quickly and dramatically turning her head away. When he asked if she would come into the office, Carla refused to enter without her mother, so he invited both of them to come in together.

Mother sat down, but Carla immediately whirled around the room and bounded over to the dollhouse. She picked up a doll and threw it against the wall of the house, then turned to Dr. G. and burst into laughter. "She's so stupid!" she shouted. She then repeated this sequence with other figures. "Stupid, stupid, they're bad and stupid!" Her sullen, angry facial expression had vanished and her grunts changed to laughter accompanied by baby-talk. At this point, Mother asked Carla if she could leave the office, but Carla paid no attention to her question. When her mother opened the door to leave, Carla was preoccupied with her dolls.

Carla continued to toss dolls and cackle hilariously after her mother left. She paid no attention to Dr. G. She first took the role of the baby in the family, babbling unintelligibly as the baby fussed and cried, then roared with laughter as she played out the mother doll spanking the baby. "Bad baby! Bad baby! You're so so bad!" she exclaimed. Carla ignored Dr. G. as he commented on how sad it was that the baby and the mother were not getting along.

After a few more moments, Carla suddenly stopped midstream and picked up a piece of drawing paper and crayons. "I'll draw a calico cat," she said. She began to draw. "I hate Barney!" she blurted out, and continued to draw. Her words and her thoughts confused Dr. G. as one idea was not logically connected to another. Carla continued this pattern of seemingly unconnected free associations that he could not understand.

While Carla drew, Dr. G. began asking her questions. He asked if she knew why her mother had brought her to see him and Carla said she had no idea. He asked her whom she played with at home and at school, and she said that she had "lots of friends and no problems or worries." When Dr. G. asked Carla about school, she said that she was in the third grade and liked school. When he asked her what she liked best, she answered, "Art and recess." Carla also said she liked eating with her friends, with whom she often shared her lunch and her lunch money. Her responses were very brief and Dr. G. had to ask her more questions to get her to give him more information.

Carla had trouble carrying on a back-and-forth dialogue on any subject. A question was first followed by "I don't know." Then Dr. G. would have to prod her to get a verbal response. For example, he asked her what she meant when she said she shared her lunch money with her friends. "I like to share my money with them," she answered.

"Why?" he asked.

"I just do," she replied.

"Do they share money with you?"

"No."

"Then I wonder why you share it with them," said Dr. G.

"I don't know." Carla answered, avoiding any eye contact. Dr. G. was unable to get beyond such brief responses. He felt that Carla was focused on her own agenda, and that he was simply intruding on her actions.

Dr. G. asked Carla if she could draw another picture and perhaps tell a story about it. She clearly enjoyed drawing and agreed to do so. She worked carefully, drawing a picture of two unicorns facing each other. Her fine motor and graphic work were excellent. After completing her drawing, she told a story:

> Once upon a time there were two little unicorns that ate a lot of grass. But one day they ate all the grass in the land. Then they had to look somewhere else but they couldn't find any. So they went to the water and died. They died, the end.

As she uttered her last sentence, Carla suddenly threw the paper and crayon into the air. "I want to play something else!" she demanded. "Let's have a tea party!" She walked over to a toy container of dishes, took out some dishes, and set one placemat for Dr. G. When she was satisfied with the setting, she went over to the tissue box, took out a tissue and carefully placed it on her outward extended forearm the way a waitperson would. "Sit down over here!" she commanded, turning to Dr. G. He sat down.

"May I take your order?" Carla asked, in a pseudo-adult voice tone.

"What's on the menu?" asked Dr. G.

"Anything you want," she replied.

"What's the best thing in this restaurant?"

Carla laughed. "Eat this mud soup!"

"Mud soup!" Dr. G. exclaimed.

"Eat it and shut up!" Carla whirled around the room laughing.

When Dr. G. said they would have to stop because the session was ending in a minute, Carla began crying out "W-a-a!" in a loud baby voice. "It's not fair!" she whined, "I make the rules!" Dr. G. told Carla that he had worked it out with her mother and he was going to see her again. "Yay!" she exclaimed in the voice of a much younger child, then clapped her hands as the session ended and they walked into the waiting room to say good-bye. Mother stood up and shook Dr. G.'s hand as they confirmed their next appointment.

In the course of this single session, Dr. G. had observed many things: Carla's high emotional, behavioral, and biological reactivity, her high intensity, her difficulties with self-control, her narrow range of emotions, and her rapid mood shifts. He also observed the difficulty that she had sustaining a two-way interaction for more than one or two back-and-forth exchanges of words. He wondered if Carla was able to process all that he was saying. Dr. G. had the feeling that Carla did not comprehend much of what he had said to her. Carla also avoided eye contact and seemed to have a lot of trouble responding to gestures and other social signals such as hand signals to slow down or smiles to try to engage her.

Carla's greatest strengths were in large muscle movement, fine motor movement, and graphic skills. She seemed unusually adept at navigating as she moved around. Despite her wild whirling about the therapy office, she didn't bump into things and she wasn't at all clumsy. Her movements had been extremely fast during the hour, yet she could sequence them instantaneously and handle objects with dexterity. Carla seemed to crave movement. Her body was in perpetual motion. When she moved about the room she laughed excitedly, but when she was sitting down, her facial expression was sober. She seemed to get overexcited quickly in the course of any activity. For example, when she started to play with the dollhouse family, her play became a wild fight between siblings. When she pretended to be a waitress, she began to lose control as she demanded that Dr. G. eat his "mud soup." Her own ideas seemed to excite her, as did playful comments on Dr. G.'s part. The smallest incident might shift her into a hyperexcited state. In addition, Carla's attention span was extremely brief; the only sedentary activity that held her attention for more than a few moments was drawing.

Dr. G. was also struck by how Carla had related to him, meeting him for the first time, and then ordering him around and commanding him to do things, heedless of his status as a complete stranger. She seemed to have no inhibitions at all.

From his brief observations of Carla and her mother before and after the session Dr. G. speculated that Ms. L. mainly tried to "keep the peace" in dealing with Carla. She reacted to Carla's excitement by remaining calm, her facial expression unchanged. Ms. L. made few distinct gestures that Carla could use as guidance for her own behavior. Ms. L.'s facial expression did not clearly reveal either approval or disapproval of Carla's actions, which left her confused.

Carla came back for two additional evaluation sessions in which Dr. G. gave her some psychological tests. She was restless and fidgety during these sessions, but she cooperated when Dr. G. gave her directions to do something. Carla had trouble staying focused. She was easily distracted by noises and looked around each time there was a noise from outside the office. She became tired quickly and needed frequent breaks during each session, when she would lie across the testing table. Even when she sat up, her body had a rag doll-like quality.

Carla's test scores matched Dr. G.'s observations, with scores consistently at the lower end of the average range. Her ideas were highly concrete and superficial. She had particular trouble responding to questions where she had to evaluate situations and make judgments. Carla seemed at a loss when she was asked how she would handle real-life situations. Her explanations showed that she didn't get the big picture, that her thought processes were piecemeal and fragmented. For example, when Dr. G. asked Carla what she would do if she found someone's wallet or purse in a store, she answered, "Just leave it where it is so they can find it." When he asked her what she'd do if a smaller girl started to fight with her, she responded, "How tall is she? I don't know her . . . hit her if she hits me first!" Carla's verbal scores on more structured tasks were a bit higher than her scores on tasks requiring more verbal fluency. She could recall facts that most children acquire through home and early school experiences, but she had trouble reasoning and solving problems.

In visual tasks, Carla seemed to take in only the big picture, missing important details. When she was shown a picture of a female face with the eyelashes missing, for example, Carla blurted out, without scanning the card, "The body's missing!" When she was shown a picture of a step ladder with a step missing, she said, "The person on the ladder." Carla didn't take time to scan different parts of the pictures; she reacted immediately to the first thing that caught her attention. However, surprisingly, when she was shown the components of a picture she could see relationships between the parts and organize them spatially. Despite her attention problems, Carla could organize partial information into meaningful wholes. For example, she had no trouble putting puzzle pieces together, or reproducing block designs using a set of blocks.

Carla had difficulty with projective story tests that involved looking at ambiguous pictures and explaining what was going on. Again, she tended to respond to details that caught her attention immediately, but she was unable to connect the details or build bridges between ideas. For example, on the first card of the Thematic Apperception Test (TAT) she responded, "A boy, a violin, and some music. He's looking at it."

"What do you think is happening in the picture?" Dr. G. asked.

"He's just looking," Carla replied.

"What do you think will happen next?"

"I don't know," she responded. "This is boring." Carla continued to label things in each succeeding picture, but she was unable to organize details into meaningful stories. She had similar problems when she was shown inkblots and asked to tell a story about them.

Carla also had trouble when asked to draw pictures of specific objects herself. When she had the opportunity to be creative and to share her ideas, her drawings were stark, and she was unable to sustain her effort. Carla quickly drew three different pictures—a house, a tree, and a person—each containing few details. Thus, on both objective and projective tests, Carla's responses consistently revealed difficulties in higher level thinking.

Some of Carla's responses on the Rorschach (inkblot) test, "a little devil" and "an ugly toad," for example, suggested possible negative feelings about herself and her ability to cope with a world populated by witches, devils, and other scary creatures. When she looked at the last card on the Rorschach, a card filled with colors and many details, Carla focused on two tiny details and exclaimed, "A crab and a scorpion, they're fighting with each other!" She had ignored the bright colors that filled the card and focused on two gray details, and Dr. G. wondered if she was describing the conflict that went on between her and her mother.

After reviewing Carla's family and developmental histories as well as his observations of Carla and her test results, Dr. G. organized the materials he had gathered using the DIR model and shared his thoughts with Carla's mother. The DIR model helped him bring together the possible biological and environmental contributors to Carla's problems and view them within a context of emotional milestones that children master on the road to emotional competence. On the biological side, Carla showed sensory reactivity, mixed sensitivities in different sensory channels, and difficulties modulating emotions.

On the environmental side, there were a number of contributors. First, Carla's mother was a single parent with no external support system to back her up and provide substitute caregiving. Ms. L.'s work schedule allowed little time with Carla to get things done. There was not enough time for chores, homework, play, and down time. Both Carla and her mother were always pressured by their schedules. At the end of the day, when Carla needed the most supervision, Ms. L.'s energy was at its lowest. Carla's unpredictable roller-coaster moods wore her mother down, and Ms. L. was thus unable to help Carla calm down when Carla was upset. In response to Carla's crankiness and tantrums, Ms. L. became progressively more upset herself, which led to escalating negative emotional cycles between mother and child. Ms. L. over-stimulated Carla by yelling and rigidly punished her by taking things away, but failed to positively reinforce Carla's behavior when she did what she was supposed to. This threw the whole rhythm of their interactions off; they were out of sync, and their anger at one another became more and more intense.

To make matters worse, at school Carla's teachers failed to understand her struggles. Their rigid handling of Carla and pressuring attempts to "make her do the work" made Carla even more unhappy. Thus, when Ms. L. picked Carla up from daycare she was often met by a child who was irritable, angry, and emotionally overloaded.

Carla's Developmental Profile

As part of Carla's evaluation, Dr. G. had Carla's mother fill out some special questionnaires that looked more closely at how she dealt with sensations and constructed her sensory profile in terms of sensory reactivity, sensory processing, sensory affective processing, motor planning, and motor tone.

Sensory Profile

Sensory reactivity. Carla had mixed reactivity to auditory stimulation. She was frequently distracted by sounds. Even background noises such as a fan or a refrigerator would annoy and distract her. At other times, she appeared under-reactive to auditory stimulation, as when she failed to tune in to what was being said to her.

Carla also seemed hypersensitive to visual stimuli. She frequently expressed discomfort with bright lights, covering her eyes or squinting, and avoiding bright sunlight.

Where touch was concerned, Carla expressed distress during grooming, was very sensitive to certain fabrics, and reacted aggressively to touch. She also had oral sensory sensitivities. She was a picky eater, especially where different food textures were concerned. She had strong preferences for crunchy foods and craved carbohydrates, particularly potatoes. When she played, she often had some non-food object or her hand in her mouth.

In contrast to her hypersensitivities, Carla was under-reactive to vestibular stimulation, which she craved, seeking out all kinds of movement activities, twirling herself, spinning and frequently finding objects she could spin on such as a swivel chair. She seemed to love the dizzy feeling she got from either whirling herself around in a chair or spinning herself to fast music. Even when Carla sat watching television, she would rock unconsciously on the couch or on the floor.

Sensory processing. In the auditory area, Carla had difficulty making sense out of long sentences and directions with many steps when they were given aloud. For example, she often seemed confused when she was told to do more than one thing at a time. In class, she became lost when her teacher began to explain things, turning away within a few moments.

Carla also had visual processing problems. She had a hard time finding objects in competing backgrounds and often could not find things in her room or drawers when they were messy. This was a source of fights because she would blame her mother for taking her possessions.

Multisensory processing was difficult for Carla. She frequently had trouble paying attention. She often looked away from tasks to notice all of the actions taking place in the room. Carla did best processing stimuli associated with hands-on experiences. She was creative in the arts and skilled in doing crafts.

Sensory affective processing. Carla had trouble reading others' emotional signals with her senses and tended to misread indicators of what people were feeling. For example, when Carla's mother spoke to her in a normal voice, giving her directions, Carla accused her mother of yelling at her. She found it especially hard to make sense visually out of others' emotional cues. Carla couldn't read facial expressions. This caused problems with other children as she was unable to recognize the visual signals that they were feeling intruded upon when she crossed their boundaries. When another child would gesture "Stop!" she would keep moving in on the child's space. Finally, Carla had difficulty decoding emotions through touch. For example, when her mother held her firmly to try to gain her attention, she thought her mother was angry with her.

Because of these processing problems, Carla failed to respond appropriately to social and environmental cues. She was often inflexible and was upset by situations that other children could handle more easily.

Motor tone. Carla's motor tone was variable. Even though she enjoyed movement activities such as dance, she tended to tire easily, had difficulty holding particular body positions such as sitting for long periods of time, had poor endurance, and frequently appeared lethargic.

Motor planning. Motor planning was an area of strength for Carla, as was particularly apparent in her skill at arts and crafts. She was able, for example, to create intricate clay figures. She was also skilled at dancing, bike riding, and other sporting activities. In addition, she could put puzzles together easily and was good at making block constructions, demonstrating her fine motor strengths.

Associated with Carla's sensory issues were modulation problems. She had a lot of trouble calming herself down. For example, when Ms. L. told Carla to stop playing and put her toys away, Carla would invariably ignore her mother's words and continue to play, which led to Ms. L. becoming frustrated and angry. When Ms. L. shouted, Carla would yell back at her and then accuse her mother of being mean without acknowledging how she had provoked this "meanness" herself.

Carla's sensory challenges affected her behavior in many ways. She tended to waste time, had difficulty getting ready to do things, and always did things the hard way. Furthermore, her sensitivities caused trouble when plans or expectations had to be changed. Carla was unable to tolerate changes in her daily routines.

Functional Emotional Developmental Levels

Along with constructing Carla's sensory profile, Dr. G. also used another scale to assess different emotional milestones and get a clear picture of Carla's functional emotional developmental levels.

Self-regulation and interest in the world. Carla was able to remain calm, focused, and organized in a highly structured one-on-one task that she was good at, like drawing, but was overly reactive, intense, hyperactive and sensation-craving when no specific instructions were given to her, as in the case of free play. She became overloaded and upset in the presence of novelty, when experiencing intense, multisensory stimulation—as in a shopping mall, for example—and when someone's expectations conflicted with her wishes. She was also upset by her own urges, as when, for example, during her first session she picked up dolls and threw them while repeating the words "stupid" and "bad."

Carla could not calm herself so as to stay connected with an adult while exploring basic emotional themes such as dependency, attachment, or empathy. Activities and behaviors intended to soothe her only seemed to upset her more. When Dr. G. slowed his pace, for example, Carla became whiny and looked for objects with which to start a new activity. Communication between Carla and Dr. G. often consisted only of erratic bursts of brief two-way volleys unpredictably disrupted by Carla's mood changes. For example, Carla and Dr. G. might be playing with the dollhouse and Carla would suddenly walk over and start pounding clay without giving any kind of signal that she wanted to change activities. Carla also had trouble regulating her emotions, discharging feelings of sadness, anger, and disappointment in toddler-like actions such as throwing things or making destructive sweeping movements with her arm across the objects she and Dr. G. had arranged. Carla had not yet learned to reflect on her feelings and to express them appropriately.

Forming relationships, attachment, and engagement. Carla evidenced brief moments of warmth and was sometimes even flirtatious, but most of the time she behaved superficially, bent solely on getting her own needs met, and held herself aloof from the adults in her life, with the exception of her mother. With her mother, she was able to be intimate and caring, but these positive feelings were disrupted by strong emotions such as anger or separation anxiety. Carla discharged strong negative emotions violently, hitting or throwing things.

Two-way purposeful communication. Carla was able to communicate briefly by means of facial expressions and basic gestures such as pointing when she wanted a need met. However, she had difficulty carrying on a continuous back-and-forth interaction with multiple gestures. She paid little attention to most of Dr. G.'s gestures and emotional signals. When Dr. G. signaled Carla to stop doing something by putting his hand up in a stop position, for instance, she ignored his gestures and continued what she was doing. To get her to stop, he had to either get in her face and say, "Hey, did you hear me?" or put his hand on her arm to physically stop her activity.

Verbally, Carla had trouble engaging in a conversation of any depth regardless of topic. When Dr. G. tried to communicate with her, her response was almost always "I don't know" or "this is boring." At home, in school, and in the therapy office, Carla had the same difficulties with intimacy. In therapy sessions, Dr. G. felt that he and Carla related to each other only on a superficial level, either because she was unable or because she was unwilling go further. When he questioned her about an idea, she quickly cut off the communication by saying, "I don't know," changed the subject, or told Dr. G. to "Shut up!" and do as he was told.

Behavioral organization, problem solving, and internalization. Carla was able to organize her behavior when she wanted to get a need met. If, for example, she wanted Dr. G. to videotape her, she could present her wishes one after the other in order to organize the activity. However, she had a lot of trouble understanding others' intentions. Because Carla tended to misread cues with adults, she was usually angry or irritable around them. She also found it hard to read other children's social cues and, as a result, few would play with her.

Carla was able to take in specific concrete facts and retain them, but she had trouble synthesizing and using information gained from her own experiences to solve problems, particularly where her social world was concerned. She knew that Columbus discovered America, for example, but she couldn't explain what she would do if she lost a ball that belonged to a friend or if a smaller girl started to fight with her. She had difficulty putting all the facts together and picturing the possible consequences of her own behaviors; in other words, she had trouble with big-picture thinking. Furthermore, she was unable to make connections between her own ideas and someone else's.

Carla couldn't accept another person's explanations for events and thus was unable to negotiate or compromise. Her thoughts related only to the immediate moment and her present need. On a structured test such as assembling puzzles from component parts, she was able to organize the pieces into a larger whole. But in the real world of her everyday experiences, Carla couldn't see how things fit together. She reacted to what was immediately in front of her without thinking about potential dangers and was unable to visualize what would happen when she behaved in an inappropriate way. Because she couldn't sequence things on her own, Carla had to be given very specific directions, one step at a time.

Representational elaboration and differentiation. Carla tended to translate her emotions into physical terms. She constantly complained about stomach aches and headaches when she didn't want to do something that an adult requested of her. Each morning, when it was time to separate from her mother to go to school, she suddenly complained of a stomach ache. When it came time to do homework, she had a headache. It was difficult for Carla to use ideas to elaborate on her feelings. Instead, she would lash out physically when she felt angry or cling to her mother when she felt anxious or needy.

Where symbolic representations were concerned, Carla appeared to experience fleeting moments of creativity and imagination, particularly in her drawings. She was able to express an idea in either words or pictures, but not to expand upon it in either mode. For example, in her story about the unicorns presented earlier, when Dr. G. tried to question Carla about why the unicorns died, she was unable to continue talking about it and instead shifted to a new activity.

Emotional thinking. Carla's thinking tended to be centered on getting her needs met. She seemed to think in an all-or-nothing, polarized manner and rarely talked about anything being good. Her world was a miserable place, pure and simple. Carla would complain vehemently that her mother never did anything for her, that she never got anything from anyone, or that she would never be able to finish her homework. She rarely used "gray" words such as "sometimes" or "maybe."

Carla had enormous difficulty describing the components of a situation one after another. She couldn't see the connection between her behavior and its results. For example, she failed to recognize that her refusal to follow her mother's directions made her mother feel frustrated and angry and that this led to her mother raising her voice and then punishing her. Dr. G. saw Carla make few connections between her actions and his responses. In response to events, she discharged emotions through actions accompanied by whining and other vocalizations, but she rarely used feeling words. Carla responded to emotional experiences with infantile outbursts that failed to differentiate one emotion from another. When she was disappointed, for example, she would become irritable, whine, and cry exactly as she did when she was angry.

Carla was able to construct only limited make-believe symbolic communications that lacked creative elaboration. Her play seemed highly constricted. The only themes around which she could organize her doll play, for instance, were bossiness or fights between siblings. When Dr. G. tried to introduce themes such as sharing and cooperation, Carla dug in her heels and told him that things were going to be done her way! Because she had trouble bridging ideas, Carla couldn't reflect on her own feelings or think relativistically, in terms of degrees. For example, she couldn't tell someone that she was getting "a little mad." Carla went from zero to an explosive outburst almost instantaneously, demonstrating that she experienced feelings only in an exaggerated, all-or-nothing form.

Carla's Treatment Plan

Carla's mother and Dr. G. formulated an individualized, comprehensive, tentative "treatment plan" that coordinated the various aspects of work needed to help her. This plan was informed by Carla's developmental profile—including sensory and modulation needs, environmental challenges, and functional emotional developmental capacities. The plan included individual therapy, parent guidance sessions with Carla's mother so that she could orchestrate a concurrent program at home, school consultation, and medication management by her psychiatrist.

As is often the case, putting Carla's tentative treatment plan into effect was difficult. Ideally, Carla needed to be seen more than once a week for the intensive work on primary issues of relating that she clearly needed. Also, Carla's mother needed weekly sessions to help her understand Carla's needs, put a home program into practice, and sustain an ongoing dialogue about Carla's functioning both at home and at school. In addition, Dr. G. needed frequent phone contact with Carla's teacher and periodic meetings with other educational professionals so as to monitor her progress in school and make changes in her school program as needed. Carla also needed weekly occupational therapy sessions to work on her sensory challenges. Finally, Dr. G. needed to work with Carla's psychiatrist to monitor her behavior while different medications or combinations of medication were being tried for her unstable moods.

Some components of this ideal plan, however, could not be implemented because of the realities of the situation. To begin with, Carla's mother worked fulltime, and the combination of her work responsibilities and the challenges of helping Carla with her schoolwork made it difficult for her to bring Carla for therapy more than once a week. She was able, however, to schedule bi-weekly parent guidance meetings with Dr. G. and to have phone contact with him between sessions. Also, Carla attended a private parochial school where the staff were resistant to outside consultation. This impeded Carla's progress and ultimately resulted in her changing schools. Scheduling made it difficult to pursue occupational therapy. However, Carla's psychiatrist was very accessible for collaborative work.

Thus, Carla's final treatment plan consisted of weekly therapy sessions, bi-weekly contact and phone contact with her mother, indirect recommendations to Carla's teacher via her mother's contact with her, and phone contact with Carla's psychiatrist.

Carla's Psychotherapy

The initial goals for Carla's individual therapy were to improve Carla's ability to pay attention during sessions and to help her learn self-calming strategies and techniques; to develop sustained chains of regulated emotional communication; and to help Carla to organize and sequence her ideas and behaviors.

Goals with Carla's mother were to help her understand her child's developmental profile, including her sensory challenges and her emotional developmental capacities; to help her identify and work with Carla's sensory differences and thus create an environment at home within which Carla might develop her skills; to teach her how to support Carla's mastery of all emotional milestones; to help her become a "co-regulator" who could help Carla learn to manage her own moods and behavior.

Because Dr. G. was unable to meet with Carla's mother weekly, he decided to structure their sessions around specific issues. Initially, this meant focusing on Carla's sensory challenges and emotional development by presenting specific observations of her functioning in the office and listening to Ms. L.'s account of events at home. Dr. G. made recommendations for Carla's mother to try at home. For example, Carla was not able to get any work done when there were distractions and Ms. L. agreed to set up a quiet area in the house. Ms. L. would also give Carla space in which to recover when she was upset rather than continue to try to talk to her. Dr. G. pointed out to Carla's mother that trying to interact with Carla when she was upset only increased her excitability rather than soothing her. Through their discussion of specific incidents, Ms. L. developed techniques for dealing with a variety of situations at home. By developing a collaborative relationship with Dr. G. in the office, Carla's mother gradually began to model Dr. G.'s empathic, supportive style of interaction and to learn how to engage Carla collaboratively at home. She learned to be a co-regulator in interactions with Carla rather than to control her or make her feel that she was being bossed. Conflict became an opportunity to problem solve together, and this reduced Carla's oppositionalism with her mother.

Initial treatment sessions with Carla focused on helping her to regulate her mood and engage with Dr. G. Often, upon arrival, Carla would refuse to come into the office. She would either cry in the waiting room or try to bolt out of the office and into the parking lot. Her safety was a critical issue during the first three months of treatment. Carla was impulsive, had poor judgment, and was unaware that she was putting herself in danger.

During the first three months, however, Dr. G. learned that when Carla was in a high energy state, if he remained calm and followed her to make sure that she was safe without becoming excited himself; she would calm down and come into the office. For example, on one occasion Carla dashed out into a torrential rain outside the building. She ran out into the parking lot and started dancing to her own rendition of "Singing in the Rain," beckoning Dr. G. to join her. When he told her that he would watch her from under the awning to make sure she was safe, she quickly lost interest, stopped, ran back into the building, dashed into the office and slammed the door behind her. Meanwhile, Dr. G. followed her back in and stopped in the waiting room to signal her mother not to intervene. After a few moments, Carla opened the office door and whined, in the voice of a much younger child, "Will you play with me?"

Despite such occurrences, however, when Carla was self-absorbed in play during a session, Dr. G. was able to enter her play by being more active, asking questions about what she was doing, and she would accept him. Before asking a question, he would cue

Carla with a gesture. For example, Dr. G. might move his arm between Carla and the toy with which she was playing, then extend his palm into Carla's visual field and make a "Stop!" gesture before asking the question. At other times, he might gently place his hand on Carla's to express his confusion about something she said or did. The "Stop!" gesture and the "I'm confused" gesture introduced the concept of two-way non-verbal communication. Soon Carla began to use a "Stop!" gesture to let Dr. G. know that he was bothering her.

During the first three months of treatment, Dr. G. worked on following Carla's lead and developing a rhythm in their interactions. He followed Carla's reaction time, her rate of verbal and motor output and her behavioral rhythm. He also paid attention to pauses in their interactions, interruptions to their play and their back-and-forth turn-taking. Carla chose what she wanted to do and Dr. G. would play along with her as a playmate. If Carla took out some dolls, Dr. G. took the part of one of the dolls and carried on a dialogue with her, for example. As they developed a rhythm, they were able to get into a natural back-and-forth, more sustained dialogue. By responding to Carla's actions but varying the pace and intensity of involvement, Dr. G. gradually helped her to remain calmer during sessions. For example, when he noticed that Carla was becoming agitated, Dr. G. would slow his pace and measure his words, thus slowing the interaction and interrupting her excitement.

In working with Carla, Dr. G. tried always to take her sensory challenges into account. Because Carla was hypersensitive to sounds, he and Carla's mother scheduled therapy sessions in the evening when no other children were in the office suite, thus cutting down on noise interference. Also, because Carla was sensitive to fluorescent lights, Dr. G. used a three-way lamp during her sessions to reduce light intensity and allow Carla to choose how bright the office would be.

They also worked on coming into the office without resistance. Whenever Carla arrived in an irritable state, Dr. G. interpreted her behavior as a message for him to keep his distance. He found that he was able to maintain two-way communication by sitting at a distance from Carla, interacting with her by slowing his rhythm, thus allowing her space and time to regulate her mood and slowly asking permission to join her. Dr. G. could accept Carla's "No!" without abandoning his attempt to interact with her, simply shifting to a less threatening approach. He also tried to create a slower rhythm by watching and waiting before commenting.

Carla's play repertoire consisted of three activities: aggressive dollhouse play, pretend cooking, and making clay ornaments. She used the dollhouse and doll figures to play out a theme in which she was the older sister and Dr. G. was the younger brother. Gleefully, she would tease Dr. G., order him around and make sure that she obtained supplies while he was deprived. Carla was the boss and Dr. G., as younger brother, had to follow her rigid rules. She could be quite aggressive in this play, hitting the younger brother dollhouse figure with the older sister doll when she became angry with him. Dr. G. made their interactions more complex by becoming a player in her play. When Carla put some toys in the sister's bedroom, Dr. G. wanted to know why she got to have all the good toys. As she continued to play with the toys, taunting the brother, Dr. G., playing the part of the brother, pleaded with Carla for a turn. By becoming a player, he was gradually able to get Carla to respond to him verbally and to begin to connect her ideas to his. Slowly, she allowed more words to be exchanged between them. Whereas their early exchanges were primarily action-oriented, Carla became increasingly willing to listen to Dr. G.'s words, to answer "wh" questions, and to share her ideas. For example, when the younger brother protested that the sister would not let him play with her toys, Carla began to say that she did not want him to play because she was afraid that he might break them because he was so young.

Once Carla was able to better regulate her emotions, Dr. G. was surprised at the range of her interests, her creativity, and her ability to sustain their interaction. During the first six months of therapy, as Carla and Dr. G. developed an attachment, he introduced a technique that had been successful with other children with self-regulation difficulties. Dr. G. suggested that they begin to make movies. Carla could choose one of her activities and they could videotape it and then watch it together. This method involved a number of high-level executive functions, which for Carla were weak. First, each week, she had to think about the activity she wanted to tape. Second, they had to make a plan to get all of the needed toys out to do the taping. Third, because they would both be on tape, Carla and Dr. G. had to negotiate giving each other a chance to talk. Fourth, to keep the movie going, they had to organize their activities into a sequence that would flow logically. Fifth, by watching the movie together, they could talk about it and see how they could improve their work on the next episode of their show. This involved paying attention to the tape, sitting together for longer periods of time, engaging in chains of emotional communication as they reviewed the tape, and reflective thinking.

Carla agreed to the idea and decided to make a "Cooking Show" that was going to be on national TV. She was the world's best cook and Dr. G. was going to be her assistant. Carla would set the agenda for the show. This activity involved big-picture thinking. Carla would get out all of the materials and write the recipe that they would teach their viewers on a large piece of paper. Videotaping enabled Dr. G. to get to know Carla better. The two of them developed a comedy routine more fully each week, which Dr. G. would start by deliberately making mistakes in reading and talking about the recipe. Carla, unaware that these mistakes were deliberate, then corrected him, and they would banter back and forth about why they had to do something her way rather than his way. Next, Dr. G. purposely made mistakes in carrying out the steps of the recipe. Carla had to pay attention to catch and correct the error when, for example, Dr. G. put in chocolate chips instead of eggs. This forced

Carla to think both logically and sequentially. Dr. G. could also incorporate basic gestures, for example holding his hand up in a "Stop!" position to show her that the audience couldn't keep up with Carla's rapid pace. Carla soon began to respond to these gestures and then started using her own gestures to signal back.

In the course of their play, Dr. G. also made statements to help Carla understand her sensory challenges. For example, when she became annoyed because he was talking too much, he commented on how his voice sometimes hurt her ears: "Too much talking bothers you. Your ears can't take a lot of talking all at one time. Did you know that about yourself?" In a number of sessions in which Carla played with dolls, Dr. G. talked to Carla about her sensitivity to touch through pretend grooming of the doll figures. Taking the part of one of the doll figures, Dr. G. often protested while brushing the doll's hair or putting on clothes, adding that people are often very sensitive to different touches because we all experience touch differently. Carla perked up and exclaimed, "I hate tickle touch." Dr. G. added that she didn't seem to mind firm touch, as when he put his hand on her arm at the end of a session, and Carla agreed that this didn't bother her. Thus, by means of pretend play, Dr. G. was able to help Carla recognize her own individual sensitivities and suggest some ways of dealing with them.

By the end of a year, Carla had come further than Dr. G. had expected. He felt that they had developed a positive relationship, and this was corroborated by Carla's mother, who reported that Carla looked forward to their sessions and even made comments about seeing Dr. G. between sessions. Carla had become able to share ideas and to engage in a dialogue in which her ideas connected with his. They could go back and forth in discussing a topic, with few "I don't know" responses. Carla's mother supported Dr. G.'s work with her own. In particular, during this time she was learning to stay verbally connected with Carla by shifting from the specific content to the form of Carla's behavior. For example, if Ms. L. was talking to Carla and Carla changed the subject, she would bring this shift to Carla's attention: "Did you notice that when I was telling you to clean up your toys you asked me if you could go outside?" or "When I asked you to set the table you walked over to the television. How come?"

Meanwhile, Carla began to use feeling words during her video-taping sessions with Dr. G. Early in the taping she might push Dr. G. with her hands if he made a mistake. As they progressed, she instead responded to his mistakes with statements such as, "You're making me m…a…d!" If Dr. G. asked why, Carla was able to use the word "because" and to build a bridge between his idea and hers. For example, she would often complain, "You're making me mad because you're not listening to me!" Carla showed an increasing ability to verbalize feelings of frustration, disappointment, and anger. "Mad," for example, was no longer a tantrum but a word. In their interactions, Dr. G. experienced much more back-and-forth communication and displays of joy, humor, and pleasure. Carla's thinking was becoming more logical and some shades of gray entered their dialogue, as when, for example, she told Dr. G. that she was getting "a little mad" at him. This more relativistic thinking helped Dr. G. to sense when he could push Carla further and when his words would result in Carla's disengaging, avoiding, or shutting down. Carla's mother also modeled gray-area thinking at home. She would tell Carla that she was getting "a little frustrated," and this helped to cue Carla that it was time to stop pushing her mother with her protests.

Carla's Home Plan

Mother and Dr. G. developed a home plan for Carla based on five principles:

1. Practice Floortime. Special unstructured time was set aside each day for Carla and her mother. During this time Ms. L. was to follow Carla's lead, and Carla might choose their activities. Ms. L. was to be a player in those activities, but not a director. She would join Carla in the activity, but not orchestrate it. Dr. G. explained that it was important for Carla to direct the activities so that she could experience pleasure as well as autonomy. He wanted Ms. L. to share Carla's attention and communicate as if she were playing ping-pong with Carla. Ms. L. was to try to pick up cues, volleying back and forth with Carla with both words and actions, and pay attention to her rhythm in the interaction. When Carla's mother was in the office with Carla and Dr. G., he modeled these patterns and identified them for Ms. L.

Because of the limited time that Carla and her mother had together, they usually spent this special time cooking meals together, shopping, taking walks, and playing board games that Carla enjoyed. While these were typical activities, the major difference was that Carla could make choices. She could choose a menu for dinner, go with her mother to the mall, or take walks or bike rides. With Ms. L. accepting Carla's choices, they could share the time without tension or pressure. Carla's mother expressed a feeling of relief because she had felt guilty when she was away from Carla for long periods of time, and now she was spending more time with Carla. In the past, she had cooked and shopped only *for* Carla, doing all the work herself. She had not considered that she could do these activities *with* Carla.

2. Spend time on problem solving. This was an entirely novel activity for Carla and her mother. Typically, when problems had come up, both Carla and Ms. L. would become locked into a cycle of anxiety, with each party attempting to gain control over the other. Anxiety was followed by escalating anger, leading to Carla getting in her mother's face and shouting back at her, which then led to Ms. L. punishing Carla. One battle, for example, involved Ms. L. trying to persuade Carla to keep her room reasonably neat. When her mother asked Carla to straighten up, Carla would promise, "After I watch my programs!" However, watching her programs put Carla into a tired, crabby mood in which she would react defiantly to any demands made by her mother. When Ms. L. had tried to set limits and to make the rule that Carla could only watch television after she straightened up, Carla would wear her mother down by protests, whining, and crying.

Dr. G. suggested that Ms. L. set aside 10–15 minutes a day to problem solve with Carla. During this time Ms. L. would bring up a problem and talk with Carla about it. The short period of time inhibited lecturing. Once the problem was identified, Ms. L. would help Carla to develop pictures of it in her mind, so that she could imagine different ways of solving it. For example, when Carla was anxious about going to school, her mother helped Carla to visualize herself in the classroom asking her teacher for help. In addition, Dr. G. talked with Ms. L. about making a "Problems Thermometer" that started with low temperatures and graduated to more moderate, then hot temperatures. Thus, those problems at the low end of the thermometer that weren't very important could be labeled "low temperature" problems and dealt with accordingly, instead of creating disproportionate responses.

For example, Carla had the undersensitivity to hot and cold that many bipolar children seem to have. She could go out in the dead of winter with short sleeves and not feel cold. Carla and her mother would get into struggles when her mother demanded that she put on her coat. Dr. G. discussed thermal undersensitivity with Carla's mother and she agreed that she could give Carla more control over her own body in this respect. When Carla wanted to go outside without a coat, rather than get into a fight, she and Ms. L. would discuss it. Carla could then talk to her mother about how she felt too warm when she wore her coat. They used this situation as a template for problem solving. Carla's mother made sure that her choices of problems to discuss with Carla were ones that didn't push her buttons, so that she would be able to discuss these situations with Carla and listen to her ideas.

Ms. L. had been afraid that if she gave into Carla's demands at all, Carla would take advantage of this and become even more demanding. Instead, Carla was able to compromise. Learning to carry on a dialogue about a problem made it easier to then work on "mild temperature problems" that required more negotiation. Homework completion, having sleepovers, and going special places were included in this category because they involved schedules and planning. These problems continue to be more difficult to resolve because of Carla's difficulty in gray-area thinking, her problem delaying gratification, and the strength of her urges.

3. Identify and empathize with the child's point of view. In the past, when Carla had a meltdown, her mother reacted negatively without trying to understanding the thinking behind the behavior. As she began to recognize that from Carla's perspective, there was an important reason for her protests, Ms. L. began to slow her reactions and try to identify what precipitated the meltdown. As a result of their problem solving sessions, Ms. L. was able to listen to Carla's point of view and to begin to verbalize that she understood where Carla was coming from. Thus, her responses began to shift from negative control and harsh discipline to reinforcing Carla's positive behaviors. Rather than exploding, Carla's mother offered her guidance by talking about different results for different actions.

4. Break down challenges into small components. Through problem solving, Ms. L. began to understand that at times she was asking Carla to do too much. Carla often felt overwhelmed when her mother asked her to "clean her room" and wouldn't know where to start. Ms. L. learned to break down such challenging tasks into steps, for example, asking Carla to get all of her toys off the floor before moving on to the next step.

5. Set clear limits. Carla's mother had tended to be vague when she tried to set limits. Statements like, "I don't like what you're doing" didn't give Carla the guidance that she needed. Ms. L. began to be more specific in terms of cause and effect, so that Carla would understand exactly what was going to happen if she engaged in inappropriate behavior.

Because Ms. L. had developed a better understanding of the biological underpinnings of her daughter's disorder, including Carla's sensory functioning, she was able to do many things to decrease the intensity of stimulation at home. For example, she prepared Carla for transitions and no longer sprung them on her. She also cut down on the number of activities they scheduled, thus giving Carla longer periods of down time. Ms. L. had learned when she could engage productively with Carla and when pressing Carla was going to be a waste of time. She also began to recognize Carla's need for gestures and visual cues because she was unable to process words spoken aloud as well as she could process visual stimuli.

As Carla's mother began to use these strategies more and more consistently, she reported that Carla was doing much better at home.

Carla's School Program

Carla's first experience in public school, before she was diagnosed with early-onset bipolar disorder, was disastrous. Her teachers saw her as an oppositional-defiant child and failed to understand her special needs. She then enrolled in a parochial school in which the staff tried to force Carla to conform to their program, making no effort to understand her individual differences. Her third school experience was in a private school for children with learning disabilities. Although this school was a much more supportive environment, the staff recognized their limitations in knowing how to deal with her severe mood swings and recommended that Carla be enrolled in a Special Education program in the public schools, where she could receive additional services not available in that private school.

Developing a program for a child like Carla is a difficult endeavor. We are still at the cutting edge of understanding severe mood dysregulation, and among professionals, teachers unfortunately often have had the least training in how to deal with extremely moody children. Carla's bipolar mood pattern severely impacted her adjustment to school. Her failures in three schools essentially turned her off to education. Getting Carla up in the morning and getting her to school was difficult for her mother. Despite having supportive teachers and a small classroom environment in several of the schools she attended, Carla was unable to function as a student on many school days. She entered the classroom, but would cry as soon as she was given an assignment and her teacher could not break through her negative mood state.

Dr. G. hypothesized that the main reason Carla couldn't function at school was that the focus was always on curriculum and performance rather than on Carla's emotional developmental needs, her sensory profile, and her learning patterns. Carla was often unavailable both cognitively and emotionally to learn. When she needed to focus on a school assignment, for example, she would be thinking about the fight she had with her mother about clothes that she wanted to wear. Carla needed teachers who understood this problem and were able and willing to help her overcome it. An ideal school program, Dr. G. believed, would focus on helping Carla to master the primary tasks of regulation, attachment, and communication along with addressing specific learning challenges.

Carla's short term memory was poor. She tended to forget things immediately after she heard them. For example, her teacher could tell the class to open their books to a specific page and Carla would have to look around at other children's books to see the page to which they were turning. After reading a very short passage, she was unable to answer questions because she failed to remember the details. Her previous teachers had not understood Carla's need for pictorial cues or multiple choice questions to cue her and another child assigned to help her stay on track.

Carla also had problems in language functioning. She had difficulty understanding word meanings, syntax, and discourse. Carla's thinking was very concrete, and she had trouble understanding abstract terms. She understood words like "cat" or "scream," but not complex ideas like "probably" or "later." For example, Carla would be confused when her teacher, while reading a story, asked the class, "What do you think will happen *next*?" Her language difficulties made it hard for her to carry on a dialogue with another child or adult, and as a result she tended to withdraw from other children and teachers in school. She needed to be placed in a classroom setting that provided many concrete, hands-on experiences rather than just abstract discussion. For example, in math, she still needed objects she could count instead of just working with numbers.

In the areas of sequential and spatial organization, Carla had a great deal of difficulty. This was evident in her not knowing what to do each day when she got to school even though her teachers had informed her of daily routines. Carla's teachers always had to give her individual attention in order to help her get organized at the beginning of the school day.

Carla struggled with understanding concepts in all subject areas. In math, for example, she had difficulty understanding how to perform basic operations. In reading, she had trouble understanding what a story was about. Carla also found problem solving difficult. She had a lot of trouble thinking logically, planning, and using a step-by-step process when she was confronted with a problem. Her teachers labeled this "impulsive" and had not recognized that Carla had problems thinking logically and sequentially. Carla needed teachers who understood difficulties with higher learning.

Finally, Carla evidenced severe problems with social thinking. She needed help in developing social language skills so as not to turn off her classmates with inappropriate behavior, skills such as sharing with others, understanding another child's point of view, and solving problems in interacting with others.

Carla's history of failure in school, as well as educators' failures to understand her needs, had made school a very painful place for

Carla. Even after she had made significant gains in her therapy sessions and at home, Carla was unable to use the new tools she had acquired to cope with challenges at school. She had enormous difficulty expressing her feelings and frustrations in the classroom.

Carla's ideal school program involved two types of goals: general goals and more specific goals. None of her previous school environments had developed a plan to address both levels. The general goals in school fit with Carla's therapy and home goals in helping her teacher to understand Carla's developmental profile, including her sensory and special learning needs, so as to provide an environment in which Carla could develop emotional and social as well as academic skills.

The ideal school program for Carla is a highly individualized, developmentally oriented program in a small classroom with a high teacher-pupil ratio. Her curriculum would center around her sensory profile and functional emotional developmental capacities and would address each of her specific learning challenges. For example, her classroom environment should have few auditory distractions or bright lights because noises and bright lights disrupted her functioning. Because of Carla's difficulties in many areas of language functioning, her curriculum should include a lot of multisensory, hands-on learning experiences rather than passively listening to her teacher talk. Because of Carla's attention weaknesses, these hands-on experiences should be colorful and exciting. Carla would also need a safe haven within the classroom where she could go when she had trouble self-regulating. In some classrooms, teachers have set up tents containing calming objects such as beanbag chairs, soft furry objects, and fidgets that children can use to help self-calm. Such an environment would be ideal for Carla.

Carla's teacher would need to be emotionally warm, supportive, engaging, flexible, and competent at setting limits. He or she would focus on helping Carla to regulate her emotions in the classroom, up regulating when Carla's attention strayed, and down-regulating when

Carla became giddy and excited. Carla needed a teacher who could empathize with her shifting moods.

To attain these goals within the classroom, Carla's strengths and weaknesses in each of these learning areas had to be defined. Thus, Ms. L. and Dr. G. would need to meet with Carla's teachers before the semester started to discuss her sensory profile, her functional emotional developmental capacities, and her learning patterns. Carla needed to be in a school setting that was receptive to collaboration with professionals from different disciplines.

Once school started, Carla's teacher needed to have frequent phone and/or e-mail contact with Carla's mother and Dr. G. in order to share strategies. It was essential that everyone be on the same page. Since Carla's mother was in a position to assess whether Carla would be available to learn on a given day, early morning contact between Carla's mother and teacher prepared her teacher for any problems before the day started.

To help educators understand children like Carla, we have been able to set up workshops within some schools to educate the teachers about sensory issues in dysregulated children. Schools have been receptive to this training because the workshop focuses on helping teachers understand the reasons for dysregulation in children as well as strategies and techniques for dealing with dysregulated children. We discuss the need for individualized, developmentally oriented curricula. We also introduce the five principles, i.e., Floortime, problem solving, identifying and empathizing with a child's point of view, breaking tasks down into small components, and setting clear limits.

Thus, the goals for school were to help Carla master each of the emotional milestones spelled out in the DIR Floortime model within the context of an individualized academic curriculum at a pace that enabled Carla to process and assimilate the material. The DIR model provided the framework, her individualized curriculum provided the context, and her sensory profile provided the information for the tools and strategies to be used in the classroom.

Carla's Medication Program

Finally, Carla's mood instability required ongoing psychiatric intervention in an attempt to find medications to stabilize her mood. Carla had been placed on medication to address her explosiveness (Clonidine), but she had become too fatigued and could not function in school. She had also been placed on stimulants and antidepressants, which destabilized her mood even further. An atypical antipsychotic medication, Seroquel, had a sedating effect and interfered with Carla's availability to learn in school.

Carla's mother sought out a psychiatrist who specialized in mood dysregulation. Her new psychiatrist then began a combination of Depakote and Lithium in order to first stabilize Carla's mood so that she could interact more calmly and be emotionally available both at home and in school. Once Carla's mood was more consistent, other problems, co-morbid ADHD, for example, could be addressed with additional medications if needed. If medication was helpful, then Carla would be more available to learn in school. Appointments with Carla's psychiatrist became more frequent as different medications were tried.

The combination of lithium and Depakote helped to stabilize Carla's emotions, and she became less irritable. In situations that typically excited her, she was able to regulate herself so that her episodes of out-of-control behavior decreased. She was able to focus her attention on homework for longer periods of time and to follow instructions better. In general, she seemed to be more receptive when adults spoke to her.

Case Outcome

After three years of regular treatment and three years of follow-up, Carla is doing much better. She has become more focused, organized, and calm, and is better able to verbalize feelings when she is experiencing stress. She is now able to sustain intimacy with others in the face of strong emotions. Even in intense moments of anger, she can remain connected to someone with whom she is angry and express her anger with words. Carla's behavior has become more purposeful and organized, and she shows a greater variety of different feelings. Whereas anger and wild excitement dominated her emotional repertoire when she first began therapy, her negative emotions have become more differentiated so that she can now articulate disappointment, frustration, and sadness. Carla also evidences positive emotions such as curiosity and pride when she experiences success in an activity.

Carla has begun to read and respond to emotional signals even when she's upset. She can stop herself before placing herself in danger. When her mother signals disapproval, Carla stops herself rather than escalating the way she used to.

Carla also shows improvement in symbolic functioning. She has clearly displayed imagination and creativity. She can now amplify or expand upon her themes during her play, working for long periods during her therapy sessions at making figures out of clay and then using the figures to play out a story.

Carla's thinking now has less of an all-or-nothing quality. Shades of gray have infiltrated her emotional expression when, for example, she says that she's getting "a little angry" or "a little bored." When she's disappointed, she can tolerate the feeling with the expectation that if she doesn't get what she wants today, she'll be able to get it another day. Thinking in shades of gray results in fewer meltdowns.

Carla's ability to think logically has improved, although she still struggles with understanding that problems may arise from multiple causes. And while shades of gray are appearing in feeling states, when Carla crosses a certain threshold of excitability she is no longer able to thinking relativistically. Thus, there is still work to be done in consolidating gains as well as developing higher level capacities. The major challenge at this point is to begin to generalize Carla's gains at home and in the therapy office into the school arena.

At present, Carla continues her multi-disciplinary treatment. All of her helpers are in place and are sticking to the DIR model as a roadmap to guide their work. They are approaching Carla's difficulties one step at a time. Though challenges continue to arise, they are getting closer to putting all of the pieces of Carla's intervention plan together. Carla starts a new school in September where the staff appear to be more flexible and receptive to her needs. By addressing Carla's needs through multi-disciplinary intervention, each participant is able to draw on the knowledge from another discipline, so that all are able to work together to help this child to live a more productive and enjoyable life.

Jimmy: A School-Age Boy with a Bipolar Mood Pattern

Case Background

Jimmy's parents, Mr. and Ms. N., brought him to see Dr. G. because they were concerned about his terrible temper and irritability. Everything seemed to set him off, and once he'd begun to rage, he could go on for hours. He would pace back and forth, wringing his hands as he screamed and yelled. When Jimmy wasn't raging, he was complaining about the many ways that everyone else tried to ruin his life: his parents refused to immediately jump when he snapped his fingers, his teachers gave him too much work, and his friends wanted to do only what *they* wanted to do. Nothing satisfied Jimmy. Meanwhile, the unpredictability of his tantrums, which occurred many times a day, kept the whole family "walking on eggshells."

Jimmy's parents found it impossible to communicate with their seven-year-old son. He seemed to want to have nothing to do with the rest of the family. Questions about his day were met with an abrupt, "I don't want to talk about it!" Any experiences he did share with his parents or older sister ended in an argument as soon as they saw things differently than he did. If his family decided to take a trip somewhere, Jimmy would always choose a different location and refuse to go with them to the place that they had chosen. If his parents or sister tried to help him with his homework, Jimmy would insist that their method was wrong and that he knew how to do the work and would do it his way. While few genuine interests could hold his attention, at times Jimmy seemed to stimulate himself by pacing, annoying his sister, or finding something to argue about. Jimmy's mother reported occasional moments of warmth, in bed before he fell asleep, for example, but these were rare. The rest of the time, Jimmy wanted everyone to "bug off!"

In spite of this, however, Jimmy was terrified of separations from his parents, protesting vehemently whenever they told him they had to leave. Jimmy was so anxious he even had difficulty going upstairs or downstairs away from other family members when they were at home. He would refuse to leave the main floor of his house without somebody accompanying him.

Jimmy's parents responded to his tantrums by trying to calm him, but this only resulted in an escalation of rage and shouts of "Stop lecturing me!" and "Leave me alone!" Instead of doing as Jimmy asked, his parents would continue to reason with him. He could use words to tell them about his angry feelings, they would insist, promising that if he did, they would listen. "You never listen!" Jimmy would scream. His parents would then become frustrated and begin yelling themselves, attacking and counterattacking. When Jimmy was adamant about not doing something, they would send him to his room. "I'm not going, you can't make me!" he would protest.

"If you don't go to your room, I'll have to take you!" Mr. or Ms. N. would shout.

"See if I care!" Jimmy would retort. When everyone was exhausted—and, at times, in tears—Jimmy would cry too, saying that he wished he could die because he made everyone miserable. Then they'd all feel guilty and apologize and the cycle would begin again.

By the time of Jimmy's first therapy session, he and his parents were at their wits' end. Jimmy's father expressed total frustration, his mother sobbed helplessly, and Jimmy himself said he thought it would be better if he weren't alive.

At school, Jimmy was constantly out of his seat and unable to work. He would get up, walk around the room, sharpen and then break pencils, and talk incessantly. His thoughts raced from one topic to another while again and again Jimmy disrupted the class and ignored his teacher's command to sit down. Even when he was sitting down, Jimmy frequently interrupted the teacher with silly noises or comments designed to make his classmates laugh. If one of his classmates tried to answer a question, for example, Jimmy would yell out that it was a stupid answer. He was the class clown, and the other children refused to play with him. Jimmy found this difficult to understand. If he thought something was funny, why wouldn't everyone else feel the same way?

Academically, he was beginning to fail. He had problems with math, hated to read, and refused to do any handwritten assignments at all. Out of frustration, he'd break his pencil points and roll his papers into balls and throw them. Jimmy told his parents he hated school because he felt retarded. Teachers called almost every day to complain to Jimmy's mother, who was afraid to leave the house for fear she'd get a call to come and pick him up.

When Dr. G. asked Jimmy's parents to describe their family history, they said that both of them had experienced depression and that there was a history of mood disorders on Ms. N.'s side of the family, including both depression and bipolar disorder. However, both parents seemed highly intelligent and successful.

Jimmy's developmental history was characterized by early health problems—hydroceles, hernias, numerous ear infections, and high fevers—but his developmental milestones were on time. However, he had extreme auditory, visual, and tactile hypersensitivities along with his mood problems. Other people's voices bothered him, bright lights annoyed him, and he was highly sensitive to different fabrics and tags on his clothing. He also became fatigued easily and had low motor tone. For example, he would frequently complain that writing assignments hurt his hand and made him tired. His gross and fine motor abilities were weak, and he avoided activities such as riding a bike or skating. His motor problems and low endurance affected his activity level. He would lie on the couch for hours mesmerized by cartoons or fixate on his Game Boy. At other times, however, he seemed to crave stimulation, becoming overexcited and silly during a movement activity.

Before he saw Dr. G., Jimmy had been diagnosed with ADHD and placed on ten milligrams of Ritalin twice a day. In response to this, he showed severe rebound symptoms, including increased activity, anger, and extremely defiant behavior. Jimmy would start pacing back and forth and refuse to cooperate if someone asked him to hang up his clothes, take his books to his room, or perform some other simple task. "You never let me just sit and rest!" he'd shout angrily. "I always have to do something for you. Why can't you do it yourself? I'm not your slave!"

When Dr. G. met Jimmy in the waiting room before their first meeting, he was seated across from Ms. N., scowling down at the floor. A thin, handsome, well-groomed boy, he was reluctant to leave his mother's side, but agreed to come into the office after she reassured him that she'd be waiting for him. Jimmy got up slowly, avoiding eye contact and refusing to shake Dr. G.'s hand when he extended it. The first thing Jimmy said after Dr. G. closed the office door was, "You might as well give up, Loser! I'm not gonna talk to you, so back off!" As he said this, he moved as far away from Dr. G. as he could and turned his back on him.

Jimmy picked up a toy, and then tossed it away. "These are stupid toys, they're for babies! You're a loser!" Jimmy's face was sullen and instead of sitting down, he paced back and forth, demanding, "Are we finished yet, Loser? Don't you see this is a waste of time? You must really be dumb!" His irritable mood continued throughout the entire session. Over and over, Jimmy complained that his time was being wasted and declared that he would not cooperate. When Dr. G. remarked that Jimmy was making it really clear that he was unhappy about being brought to see him, Jimmy snapped, "Shut up!" covered his ears, and looked away. When Dr. G. tried to engage Jimmy in conversation about home and school, Jimmy lashed out that it was "none of your f------ business!"

Toward the end of the session, Dr. G. told Jimmy that he believed his parents were not going to stop trying to make things better for him. Jimmy had already been to another therapist, and now he was seeing Dr. G. If they could not begin to work things out here, his parents would continue to seek help. Jimmy seemed to soften momentarily, saying, "Nothing will ever help me. Why won't they just leave me alone?"

"Because they're very worried about you and they love you," Dr. G. replied.

Jimmy stood quietly as he continued. Dr. G. told Jimmy that he'd like to see him again, and that he wanted to do some testing to find out what things he could do well and what things made school hard for him. "Are you trying to find out if I'm dumb or something?" he asked.

"I might find just the opposite," Dr. G. replied.

"Sure, I doubt it!" Jimmy responded, looking defeated. "My parents are only wasting their money."

When Jimmy left the office, Dr. G. felt emotionally drained. His entire body felt tight and apprehensive, a feeling he had often experienced when he believed a child might become destructive or combative. He wondered if they'd have to go through this same scene again. Would Jimmy's comments about the futility of their work together turn out to be accurate?

However, when Jimmy came back the next week, although he was still irritable, he cooperated with the testing. The tests showed that he had superior verbal ability, with a rich, expressive vocabulary and a wide fund of general information. When Dr. G. asked Jimmy to define the word "cow," for example, he stated that it was an animal that was part of the mammal family. Jimmy showed a precocious ability to think abstractly. When Dr. G. asked him how a telephone and a radio were alike, he responded that they were both means of communication rather than simply saying that they were both electric or "things you hear on," as a typical seven-year-old might.

At the same time, however, Jimmy had problems with non-verbal tasks. He had trouble focusing and sustaining visual attention and was inconsistent on tasks involving visual imagery and visual-spatial organization. For example, he had a lot of difficulty assembling puzzles. He also had trouble reproducing abstract block patterns even when a model was in plain sight. He moved the parts quickly and without a plan, taking no time to think about what the final designs should look like. In scanning, Jimmy tended to see only the big picture and missed important details. The tests, along with his behavior, reflected his tendency to act impulsively, ignoring the possible consequences of his actions.

Jimmy's drawings reflected major problems with graphomotor control. As soon as Dr. G. asked him to draw, he quickly became much more irritable and said the task was "stupid." His drawings were poor, shapes were distorted, and he had trouble connecting parts of designs. Also, his drawings showed signs of intense emotions and control issues. They were large, showing heavy pencil pressure, with several collisions between figures.

When Dr. G. asked Jimmy to make up stories about a series of pictures, he could not do this; he merely listed a series of discrete details without connecting them in a narrative plot with a beginning, middle, and end. For example, on a card depicting a farm scene, Jimmy named what each of the figures was doing, "There's a guy with a plough, a woman standing by a tree, and a woman holding books, and I don't know what they're doing." This was surprising, given Jimmy's verbal strengths on other tests.

Jimmy's Developmental Profile

After reviewing his findings with Jimmy's family, Dr. G. organized Jimmy's history, his observations, and his test data according to the DIR model. Jimmy's profile was abstracted from his parents' reports, individual therapy sessions, observations of Jimmy and his parents playing together, testing, and school reports.

Sensory Profile

Dr. G. constructed Jimmy's sensory profile after assessing him for sensory reactivity, sensory processing, sensory affective processing, motor planning, and motor tone.

Sensory reactivity. Jimmy became quickly became upset and mentally disorganized when he was overloaded with visual, auditory, and tactile sensations and when he felt challenged by others. When his parents tried to calm him, however, he responded paradoxically; he'd become more irritable and disorganized, not less. Jimmy refused to allow his parents to touch him and would cover his ears to block out their words.

Jimmy's baseline temperament was irritable. He nearly always appeared tense and "on guard," and his parents complained that they were constantly "walking on eggshells." They had learned that anything they said could lead to an argument. When Jimmy felt in control of a situation, he was able to contain his irritability, but when he was frustrated or had to respond to others' limits, he immediately began to lose it. With the exception of tuning out while focusing on his Game Boy or being with his mother at bedtime, Jimmy was unable to be calm and attentive at the same time. He always reacted intensely when overloaded. Noises bothered him, fabrics irritated him, and bright lights upset him. At even very low levels of sensory or interpersonal stimulation, he became emotionally overloaded and misbehaved.

Sensory processing. Jimmy's sensory pattern included shifting states. At different times he might be either under-reactive, appearing to tune out environmental input—when, for example, he was fixated on his Game Boy and failed to respond to his mother's or father's voice—or overreactive, becoming, in response to sensory stimulation, overexcited, and disorganized and pacing rapidly back and forth and flapping his hands to discharge excess energy. Rarely was he calm, alert, inactive, and attentive.

Sensory affective processing. Jimmy had difficulty processing emotional information with all his senses. He misinterpreted his parents' tones of voice and pitch, believing that they were angry with him most of the time and also misread facial expressions and gestures, failing to regard his mother's stroking him as a form of affection.

Motor tone. Jimmy's motor tone was poor. He tended to tire easily, especially when he was standing or holding a particular body position. His grasp was weak, and at times he complained of having no energy. His low endurance and poor motor tone interfered with his developing skills that are prerequisites for social success during childhood. Jimmy avoided activities such as learning to ride a bike, and this isolated him from other children.

Motor planning. Jimmy's motor planning was extremely weak. He avoided playing baseball, for example, because he had difficulty catching a ball and hitting. He also had trouble tying his shoes and buttoning his clothing, and this caused him great shame.

Jimmy's sensory processing problems made it particularly difficult for him to interact calmly with others. Intense emotions threw Jimmy off balance, and attempts to soothe only added fuel to the fire, upsetting him further. This was particularly evident in situations involving limit-setting and power-struggles. When Jimmy's mother offered to sit with him while he struggled with homework, for example, instead of finding this comforting he would become more anxious.

Functional Emotional Developmental Levels

Self-regulation and interest in the world. Jimmy had extreme difficulty self-regulating. His temperament was naturally irritable, and his strongest emotions were negative, irritability quickly changing to agitation. On an emotional scale from low (1) to high intensity (8), Jimmy could go from 1 to 8 almost instantaneously. He often experienced intense negative feelings when others didn't see the world in the same way as he did. For example, if Jimmy wanted a particular comic book, he couldn't understand why he had to wait to get it. He believed that any time he wanted something, others should get it for him right away. Jimmy's emotional intensity and slow emotional recovery time interfered with his ability to sustain his attention. These problems made it difficult for him to cultivate any interests. He had few hobbies or friendships and refused to participate in play activities with other children.

Forming relationships, attachment, and engagement. Jimmy had a lot of trouble with intimacy. He tended to remain aloof and isolated from family members and peers, and it was hard for him to form friendships. Jimmy also showed signs of insecure attachment. He would become anxious and clingy when his parents wanted to go out for dinner without him, for example. Jimmy was able, however, to demonstrate warmth around bedtime when one of his parents would lie in bed with him and read him stories. These were the only moments, according to his mother, when Jimmy showed pleasure, comfort, and dependency on others.

Many of Jimmy's interactions with others took the form of power struggles, during which he tried to bully other family members. They were not chains of respectful negotiation between two people, but asymmetrical battles in which, responding to a parent's simple reminder that it was time to start his homework, Jimmy would immediately snap back, "I don't want to!" or "It's too hard!" and the struggle would begin.

Two-way purposeful communication. Jimmy's communications all centered around getting his own needs met. He could be extremely calculating in manipulating his parents to buy things or do things for him. Jimmy was unable to engage in long, smooth chains of communication in order to ask directly for what he wanted or express loving feelings. He could initiate a connection around anger and aggression, but even these communications were almost immediately broken as Jimmy disintegrated into a rage. Jimmy could not read his parents' "calm down" gestures, their empathic facial expressions or hand signals to lower his voice, nor could he signal his parents to back off in a way that they understood. The rhythm of Jimmy's interactions with others consisted of only one, two, or three links before the chain was broken by Jimmy shutting down or becoming defiant. When his parents or sister said good morning, Jimmy would answer, "What's so good about it?" If they responded that it was a "new day," he would shout, "Leave me alone!" and end the conversation. Jimmy simply had not developed the capacity for long chains of smooth, regulated, reciprocal emotional communication, and this made genuine intimacy difficult for him.

Behavioral organization, problem solving, and internalization. This was an area of severe weakness for Jimmy, who tended to distort the intentions of others in his mind. He misread facial expressions and gestures and, consequently, was always suspicious of others' motives. Jimmy continually complained about his parents mistreating him and loving his sister more than they loved him. He was angry most of the time. Jimmy also misinterpreted others' tones of voice, believing, for example, that people were yelling at him when they weren't. He was unable to decode his parents' signals relating to safety vs. danger, approval vs. disapproval, or acceptance vs. rejection.

Jimmy became disorganized when experiencing intense emotions and was unable to think about solutions to problems. When he was angry, he was unwilling to negotiate. If he couldn't have his way, he refused to consider other solutions to the problem. His sole solution to most problems was that he should get what he wanted.

Representational elaboration and differentiation. Jimmy's capacity for representational and symbolic thinking was severely compromised. It was striking how a child could display superior intelligence on a test and yet be unable to play creatively or express his ideas in an organized thematic sequence. Jimmy showed no interest in pretend or imaginative play. He continually complained about being bored, but would reject any suggestion that his parents made, spending his free time exclusively on comic books and his Game Boy.

Jimmy had great difficulty symbolizing his feelings in terms of his various senses. His emotional language was one of discharge, impulse, and unregulated action: pacing aimlessly, breaking things, or sarcastically mimicking others' words. Jimmy was unable to free himself from the pressure of his urges and reacted to physiological shifts in his body automatically by blowing off steam into dramatic actions.

Jimmy had trouble using words to express either positive or negative feelings; instead, he acted his emotions out in an intense, disorganized fashion. He had not yet learned to experience an emotion, to create a multisensory image in his mind of an emotional experience, and to express it appropriately through gestures. Many of Jimmy's emotions had the same quality of intense, undifferentiated bursts of energy, whether positive or negative. If he was happy, he became oversilly without realizing that others were seeing his behavior as inappropriate; when he was sad, he would cry for long periods of time, unable to be consoled; when he was angry he would storm around the house cursing everyone and everything; and when he was scared, he clung physically to his parents, refusing to do anything unless they stayed close by. While Jimmy had other strengths, such as being able to defeat enemies on the computer, his social skills were uniformly weak.

Emotional thinking. Jimmy was an all-or-nothing thinker, and at times his thinking was totally illogical. For example, if his mother told him that she couldn't take him to buy a comic book, Jimmy's refrain was "You never get me anything! You don't care about me anyway!" He was unable to consider that perhaps his mother was involved in another task or the request was made at an inopportune time. Jimmy was not able to reflect on another person's emotions: if someone else had feelings about his behavior it simply didn't matter. Jimmy would state emphatically that he didn't care what the other person felt. "That's their problem," he said, "and if they want something to be different they should do something about it!" In addition, Jimmy was unable to identify gradations of feelings. One could not be "a little mad" or "a little disappointed." Emotions only included extreme polarities, e.g., "You hate me and I'll never get it!"

While Jimmy displayed rage dramatically, his expression of other emotions was constricted. He rarely expressed positive feelings such as pleasure, affection, or curiosity. He even expressed anger, disappointment, or sadness, in a rigid fashion: by having a tantrum instead of talking. Jimmy had difficulty reflecting on himself and others. He couldn't think about a problem having many possible causes or recognize different degrees of feelings, but would make the same extreme negative statement over and over: "You never get me anything, you never get me anything!" These difficulties resulted in relationship problems and also compromised Jimmy's use of his superior intellect in school.

In summary, Jimmy was having significant difficulty mastering his functional developmental capacities. He had trouble regulating his feelings and desires so as to calm himself down and pay attention. Jimmy had severe problems engaging, either gesturally or verbally, in long chains of back-and-forth communication with others. He was unable to reflect upon his feelings and communicate them to others with words. He had not developed the ability to symbolize his feelings, and as a result, whenever he experienced a negative emotion he immediately discharged it by blowing off steam through crying, yelling, or slamming doors. While Jimmy had verbal and abstract thinking strengths, he had difficulty using these socially.

Jimmy's parents were at a loss over how to deal with Jimmy's behaviors. They were confused about the nature of his disorder, and their confusion resulted in their trying many different interventions—talking calmly, yelling, physical action, trying to negotiate, giving Jimmy choices, taking away privileges—at different times. When one intervention was unsuccessful, they tried something else. Their inconsistency, in combination with Jimmy's inconsistencies, threw the whole family off balance. Attempts to soothe Jimmy were unsuccessful because he was overreactive to any input when he was in an upset state. Attempts to ignore him resulted in rages, as did getting into power struggles with him. Jimmy was unable to learn to soothe himself both because his inner sensations, urges, and impulses were so intense and because his parents' strategies were so inconsistent.

At school, Jimmy's teachers didn't understand what they were seeing when he disobeyed and disregarded their limits. Jimmy had a kindergarten teacher who was sensitive to his changing behaviors, and who was flexible in dealing with him, but in first grade, as academics were introduced, his teacher responded very differently. Jimmy's learning challenges led to defensive behaviors on his part that his teacher treated in ways that upset him even more, leading to even more misbehavior. Jimmy was confused because he couldn't do a lot of things as easily as other children. When he became anxious, he didn't have the tools to accept help, and his response to anxiety was to run away or create a situation where his teacher would remove him from the room.

Jimmy's Treatment Program

Jimmy's problems required both biological and environmental interventions. Treatment had to address his functional emotional developmental capacities as well as his individual sensory profile, and must be intensive, comprehensive, and multi-disciplinary. It also had to be individualized, developmentally-based, and family-oriented.

The DIR model addressed each of these dimensions. By using Jimmy's diagnostic profile, Dr. G. was able to develop a comprehensive treatment program to meet Jimmy's specific needs. Jimmy's treatment program included individual psychotherapy as well as joint sessions with Jimmy and each of his parents; parent guidance sessions to develop management strategies at home; participation in a parent support group; work with Jimmy's teachers to help them understand Jimmy's disorder and how to help him function within the classroom; consultations with occupational and physical therapists regarding Jimmy's sensory and motor challenges; and collaboration with a psychiatrist for medication monitoring.

Jimmy's Psychotherapy

The goal of Jimmy's psychotherapy was to help him develop higher level functional emotional developmental capacities. Because he had so much trouble calming himself and sustaining attention, the first order of business was to help Jimmy engage in regulated, sustained chains of back-and-forth communication. Jimmy's irritable mood kept other people at a distance and interfered with a sustained mutual exchange on almost any subject. Therefore, in their early sessions together, Dr. G. monitored Jimmy's irritability level and rhythm and used gestures and words to help him modulate his emotions, thus introducing him to a new "dance." Whenever Jimmy became irritable, Dr. G. purposely slowed his pace, spoke softly, used few words, and remained calm. This caused Jimmy's emotions to diminish in intensity. If Jimmy got blustery when Dr. G. asked him about school, Dr. G. slowly and empathically reflected that it was not something that Jimmy wanted to talk about. Jimmy was used to people reacting quickly and negatively to his blustering, and when Dr. G. reacted differently, this threw Jimmy off balance. He needed additional time to think about how to respond, which provided a short period of delay that down-regulated his behavior. Thus, he experienced a momentary, unexpected feeling of calm that could then be expanded.

Whenever Jimmy withdrew, Dr. G. actively initiated contact, quickening his pace and speaking more loudly and intensely. For example, when Jimmy brought a book into the session and sat tuning Dr. G. out, Dr. G. moved closer, deliberately looked curious, glanced up at Jimmy's face and said, "Hmm, looks pretty interesting, what's it about?" Although they couldn't yet sustain an extended interaction around a specific topic, Jimmy and Dr. G. were beginning to establish an interactive pace and rhythm that shifted from a topic of conversation to a comment on what Jimmy was doing behaviorally. For example, if Dr. G. asked Jimmy a question about something, and Jimmy retorted that it was none of his business, Dr. G. might answer, "Your words are telling me that you want to keep your information to yourself right now."

Then Jimmy would unwittingly help Dr. G. extend the exchange by saying, "That's right!" Every comment he made allowed Dr. G. to prolong their exchange by adding one more gesture and one more comment, with isolated opportunities to explore a feeling momentarily. For example, when Jimmy continued," I don't want to talk about it!" Dr. G. replied, "You seem a little annoyed. What does that feel like?" Jimmy began to make comments such as, "It makes my face feel hot!" or "I want to make a fist!" in order to make Dr. G. stop asking so many questions.

Jimmy was able to make significant gains in understanding gestures, facial expressions, and emotional communication when his mother was in the office. When Ms. N. was there, Jimmy typically positioned himself on the floor next to her chair and would play with two objects in his hand, usually puppets or plastic human figures that he would engage in a quiet, non-verbal pretend fight. Fidgeting with these objects seemed to help Jimmy organize his thoughts, focus his attention and listen to his mother, who spoke in a gentle voice and at a slow, reflective pace. At first Jimmy listened without saying anything. However, he watched his Ms. N.'s facial expressions attentively as they changed. Over time, Jimmy began to make comments about these expressions. For example, in one session she became teary as she talked about how sad she felt over not being able to talk to Jimmy about his day in school. Jimmy startled and blurted out, "What's wrong?" Ms. N. used the word "sad" as she repeated what she had just told Dr. G. Quietly, she was modeling the connection between a facial expression and a word.

In a later session, Ms. N. became more animated as she used the word "scared" to label her feeling about Jimmy's out-of-control behavior. Looking up with surprise, Jimmy said, "You mean you're really scared of me?" When his mother said she was, he put his hand on her arm and said, "But Mom, I would never hurt you, you should know that!" "But I don't know that," she replied. This opened the door to an extended back-and-forth exchange about her fearful feelings. Exchanges about feelings enabled Jimmy and his mother to develop an understanding of each other's emotions as signals to change behaviors. Jimmy had not considered that his behavior could evoke a feeling in another person. This was a new idea for him to think about. In addition, connecting specific experiences with feeling words gave Jimmy practice in symbolizing his own emotions, something he was already learning in individual sessions with Dr. G. He could get a picture of the experience in his mind along with a picture of an emotion.

A major change occurred when in one session Jimmy tried to tell his mother that when he was mad he wanted to be left alone. "When I'm mad I yell, 'Leave me alone,' but you don't!" he exclaimed. "I'm mad! Leave me alone! You only make it worse when you don't." Ms. N. said that when she saw Jimmy raging she had an "I-want-to-do-something-to-fix-it feeling!" She told Jimmy that she wanted to get closer to him and help him to calm down. He explained that when she didn't give him space, it just made him madder so that he wanted to yell. "My body feels like I want to explode!" he said. "I feel it all over my body!" Ms. N. said that she had no idea that was the way he felt and she was so happy that Jimmy could tell her. Understanding this, she agreed to give Jimmy space when he was angry.

In response to Jimmy's comments about his mad feeling, Ms. N. described a parallel experience. When she was feeling frustrated or mad, Jimmy tended to become more clingy. She gave him some examples of when he would not leave her alone when she had asked him to. She, too, needed space when she was upset. Together, they agreed to give each other space at such times. When Jimmy told his mother to leave him alone, she agreed to go into another room, and when she asked Jimmy to leave her alone Jimmy would also go to another part of the house.

The following week, Jimmy's mother described a "dramatic, exciting shift" in their interactions. They had each followed through on their agreement and the week had gone much more smoothly.

As Jimmy became better able to sustain an interaction and remain calm, he began to take chances, talking about a number of emotional issues that he had avoided, such as his scary feelings that he would eventually be sent away because of his behavior, his confusion about how people could care about him when he treated them so badly, and, most important, his belief that he was a loser who would never be able to succeed in school, hold a job, or get married and have a family. Jimmy had previously avoided each of these topics because he was afraid that sharing his fears aloud would cause them to be realized. "If I tell you these things, then you'll think about them, and maybe do it," he shared with Dr. G. and Ms. N. By verbalizing these important themes, he got feedback that gave him a new understanding of his situation.

In addition, Jimmy learned something about his sensory differences. He learned that there was a reason why he covered his ears in the presence of loud noises and that people had different sensitivities to sound. Jimmy thought that everyone heard noises in the same way. The idea that some people could be more sensitive to sound than others was new to him. Jimmy also began to understand his sensitivity to touch. He learned that people reacted differently to touch and that some people, like him, hated a soft gentle touch as compared to firm pressure.

Thus, the concepts of over-sensitivity and over-reactivity became connected to concrete experiences in Jimmy's mind and began to have meaning for him. Jimmy now understood that when he was in an out-of-control state and someone tried to help him, he couldn't tolerate their words or touch stimulation, and they would upset him rather than calm him down. Jimmy already knew that he had to be given space when he was upset, but now he understood why. By paying attention to his body signals, he was able to remove himself from situations that overloaded him. When he felt himself wanting to pace and yell, he could go to his room to calm down. This helped him both at home and at school. Jimmy was able to leave a situation that was making him feel uncomfortable and understand that adults would appreciate his self-care rather than punishing him.

As Jimmy became able to regulate his emotions and engage in back-and-forth communication, the main goal of treatment shifted to helping him symbolize his feelings with mental images. By introducing a feeling word or phrase, such as "You look sad today, like something is troubling you," Dr. G. tried to help Jimmy connect the word to a mental picture, creating symbols which enabled him to reflect on past, present, and future. Jimmy stated that he never thought about the future, saying, "I live in the now and don't think about what will happen later. It's not important to think about the future—that's not my problem!" Dr. G. stated that boys and girls often create pictures in their minds that help them connect the past, present, and future. By creating pictures, children can figure out what might happen when they do something. The picture helps them to work on a plan. He said that Jimmy often had trouble think-ing about what would happen after he behaved in a certain way. Instead, he reacted immediately and then complained later when he was given consequences that he hadn't pictured in his mind. Jimmy understood the concept of "a picture" because he could picture some things in his mind like a new Game Boy program that he wanted. As a result of these discussions with Dr. G., Jimmy began to picture situations in his mind and to think sequentially. He began to imag-ine what led to what, and to understand that there was a "before," a "now," and an "after." He was increasingly able to picture a series of events that he had initiated with his behavior and understand why an adult responded in a particular way. He did not simply assume that adults were always picking on him.

Jimmy also began to think about there being various reasons—not just one—for having a feeling. For example, he was able to see that his mother's or father's short temper when he asked for some-thing might be related to Mr. or Ms. N. having a bad day instead of automatically assuming that he had caused it. Also, Jimmy began to express degrees of feelings. He was "a little" mad at his mother for not getting him a new comic but it wasn't "such a big deal" if he had to wait for another day to shop with her.

Jimmy's Home Plan

Jimmy's work in therapy was complimented by a home program and by a physical therapy program. The components of his home pro-gram included setting up special time in which he could share ac-tivities with his father and mother that he enjoyed. Special time was set aside each day for Jimmy and each parent. For example, Jimmy got enormous pleasure from wrestling with his father, and they were able to build "wrestling time" into their schedule. Jimmy and Mr. N. had special time when they went down to the playroom to practice wrestling moves that Jimmy had seen on television.

The family also took ten minutes each day to talk about problems that had come up during the day. This was different from the special time in which Jimmy could take the lead and choose an activity. During problem solving time, any family member might bring up a problem and all agreed that they would pay attention and talk about it. Both of Jimmy's parents worked on being empathic and listening to Jimmy's point of view when he brought up something that was bothering him. Jimmy had the opportunity to give his side of the story so that his parents could better understand where he was coming from. He began to make statements like "I don't see it the same way that you do."

Another important component to the home program was breaking down challenging situations into smaller parts. Dr. G. described Jimmy's meltdowns to his parents as signals that he was feeling emotionally overtaxed. When his parents observed this behavior, they understood that Jimmy was feeling that a problem was too big for him to tackle, and they broke it down into smaller parts. This chunking strategy was used for activities such as homework or cleaning up his room.

Finally, limit-setting was an important component of Jimmy's home program. Dr. G. recommended that Jimmy's parents try to set limits that were clear, consistent, predictable, and connected to a specific event, instead of vague, open-ended, and arbitrary limits. For example, "Don't do that again" was changed to "When you do that, this is what I will do."

Jimmy's parents worked hard not to give into his provocations and shifting moods. When Jimmy shifted into an upset state, they focused on dealing with it calmly so as not to rev him up. Dr. G. suggested such remarks to them as, "This is not the time to talk about it" or "I need some time to think about that." Jimmy's parents also worked on sequencing and scheduling to make Jimmy's life more predictable for him. They provided him with a daily calendar of events so that Jimmy knew what he would be doing after school and helped him get a picture of a timeframe in his mind. They also worked on giving him definite answers to questions when he asked if he could have something. Rather than giving him an indefinite answer, they often tried to state a specific time when they would be able to meet a request.

The final component of Jimmy's home program was dealing with homework. This had been a difficult area to negotiate with Jimmy. His mother knew that when he came home from school he was emotionally spent from the day and could not sit down to do homework. At the same time, however, putting off the homework invariably led to a battle after dinner because Jimmy was too tired to do the work. If Jimmy's parents pushed him, the result was combat and rage. However, when Mr. and Ms. N. gave up and did not push, Jimmy was literally up all night, as he could not go to sleep without having finished his homework.

Dr. G. recommended a contract in which Jimmy could make a schedule showing when he would do his work. He could do all of the easy work after a snack break when he got home, then he could play. Jimmy's parents would be available to work with him on what was left after dinner. By breaking up the work into two parts, Jimmy did not feel so overloaded, and the task became more manageable.

Parent Support Group

In addition to psychotherapy and parent guidance, Jimmy's parents also participated in a support group for parents of children with severe emotional regulation problems. In this group, they were able to find other parents who shared similar experiences—parents who truly understood the anguish of raising a child with extreme mood instability and the feeling of being provoked to out-of-control behavior in dealing with a highly oppositional child. They could discuss how they managed Jimmy's behaviors and receive feedback from other parents, who also shared their successes and failures. Moreover, they could express intense, painful feelings—for example, horrible guilt about sometimes feeling unable to show love for their child—without fear of being criticized. Other parents could understand their rage, anguish, despair, and shame. The parent support group was an enormously powerful source of unexpected strength to Jimmy's parents.

Jimmy's School Program

Jimmy's parents recognized that Jimmy could not function in a traditional classroom environment with other children moving about, a large group size, and the teacher's presentation paced to the average child. In the classroom setting, he was also quickly overloaded by sights, sounds, movement, and transitions. In addition, Jimmy had specific academic challenges in math, reading, and handwriting. In the course of their work with Dr. G., Jimmy's parents decided to transfer him to a private school for learning disabled children, where he was placed in a classroom with only five other children and was able to work at a pace that did not overload him. Jimmy needed an individualized program that took into account his sensory profile and learning patterns as well as his level of development.

Jimmy's principal, teacher, and school social worker in this new school welcomed input and were willing to schedule meetings to monitor Jimmy's progress. The school staff understood the importance of modifying Jimmy's curriculum on an as-needed basis. There were times during the school year when Jimmy became depressed and was not emotionally available to learn. During the late fall and early winter Jimmy had the most trouble concentrating on the work. His teacher understood that his changing mood was a part of his biology, and she was able to be flexible in adjusting to his shifting emotional states. Dr. G., Jimmy's teacher, and Jimmy's parents worked together to develop a school program that addressed his specific needs.

The small class size in itself met many of Jimmy's sensory needs. There were far fewer distractions competing for Jimmy's attention, and his individualized curriculum enabled him to move at his own pace. When he had trouble, he was able to move more slowly as activities were broken down into smaller components. Thus, Jimmy had the opportunity to gain a sense of mastery while working at a level that enabled him to continually succeed. Jimmy's feelings of success were clearly evident as he began to talk enthusiastically about school and was upset if he had to miss a school day for any reason. This was a dramatic change from his dread of school in the past. Jimmy's mother was also invited to discuss her observations of Jimmy whenever something had happened in school to upset him. The communication between home and school provided continuity and facilitated Jimmy's emotional regulation.

Jimmy's teacher, Ms. Q., was empathic and flexible, yet firm in setting limits with him. Ms. Q. was highly attuned to Jimmy's body language, facial expressions, and gestures. When she sensed that Jimmy was having difficulty, she allowed him to put his work aside rather than pushing him to get it done, as other teachers had. This took a lot of the pressure off Jimmy, and as he was now more motivated to succeed, he would always try to get the work done. In a conference, Ms. Q. remarked that she could see Jimmy work through upset states on his own and then return to work.

Jimmy's teacher welcomed collaboration with Dr. G. to help develop strategies to meet his learning challenges. For example, Jimmy had difficulty sustaining his attention for long periods of time. Dr. G. and Ms. Q. discussed shortening his work segments and allowing him time to discharge energy before returning to a task. They also considered incorporating some of Jimmy's interests into the curriculum. As Jimmy made progress in therapy, they learned that he had interests in Japanese culture that developed from his enjoyment of Pokemon and a strong interest in dramatics that had previously been misused in his playing the role of the class clown. Now Jimmy could receive appreciation for his humor by sharing his humorous ideas with the class more constructively. When Jimmy blurted out a comment, he was not criticized; instead, his teacher found ways to respond empathically, understanding that there was a reason why Jimmy was making the comment at that specific point in time.

Jimmy has now completed two years in the program and has thrived with the support and understanding of the staff. While there continue to be problems about Jimmy's incessant talking in class and about doing his homework, a dialogue has been created to continue work on these issues. Jimmy's teacher recognizes that change is a process, and she is able to manage his behaviors more effectively by using words to tell him what she is observing about his behavior. For example, "You're doing your work very slowly today—it looks like you're thinking about something else."

Jimmy had significant motor challenges that had to be addressed because they affected other areas of his life. Not being able to ride a bike at age seven, for example, isolated him from other children, and Jimmy himself said that when he was unable to do things that other children could do, it made him feel defective. Thus, a comprehensive physical therapy program was developed to address Jimmy's gross motor challenges. He was able to work individually with a physical therapist, and his mastery of gross motor skills gave him more confidence and the willingness to take appropriate risks in order to master new skills.

Jimmy's Medication Program

Jimmy's medication intervention program made his treatment extremely complex. His psychiatrist first prescribed stimulant medication to help with his distractibility, inattention, and impulsivity. However, rather than helping Jimmy to become more organized, this only increased his hyperactivity. The psychiatrist also prescribed an anti-depressant to stabilize Jimmy's mood, but it had the opposite effect, as is not unusual for young children with bipolar patterns. Jimmy's aversive response to these medications initiated a nightmarish journey in which his psychiatrist tried many medications, including mood stabilizers—medicines typically used for bipolar disorder—none of which were successful. Finally, toxicity to a mood stabilizer forced Jimmy's psychiatrist and parents to take him off all medications.

Jimmy remained, however, on a program of Omega-3 fatty acids, a cutting edge treatment for bipolar patterns. As yet, there are no large-scale studies of the effects of Omega-3 fatty acids in either the child or adult literature, but clinical work using them with individual children as well as adults has shown promising results.

Jimmy has remained stable on the Omega-3s for more than a year and a half at the time of this writing. Within this period Jimmy has had to weather intermittent fluctuations in mood, but he has become remarkably articulate at reporting changes in his mood states and is his own best advocate due to his greater ability to use words to share his inner experiences. Jimmy can now state specifically, for example, that he feels irritable, and he can expand upon this by connecting the irritability to a specific event that happened during the week. Or, if he can't pinpoint a specific event, he'll say that a number of different things could have made him feel this way and talk about the possibilities.

After three years of treatment, Jimmy, age ten, has made dramatic changes. His ability to sustain these changes and reflect on his experiences and feelings even during periodic mood shifts is encouraging. Jimmy's therapy sessions have taken on a more mature tone as he explores many different problem areas, using words to articulate feelings and sustain a dialogue even when Dr. G. introduces difficult topics that Jimmy used to avoid. Jimmy has begun to ask questions about himself such as "How did I use to act in therapy?" He has difficulty recalling his severe emotional outbursts and even was able to laugh when his mother told him how he behaved earlier in the therapy. In sessions, Dr. G. continually makes positive connections between old behavior and new behavior to underscore the changes that Jimmy has made.

Jimmy has become a warm, humorous, and engaging young boy. His parents have been amazed at his reflective thinking. When Jimmy behaves inappropriately, he is able to consider the reason for the inappropriate behavior and go through one "maybe it was because . . ." after another. Jimmy no longer uses blame as a primary mechanism of defense. He has learned that he can do something wrong and talk about it openly.

One problem that Jimmy is still experiencing is his talkativeness in school, which relates to his ADHD. Jimmy chatters in class, and often his chatter annoys others. When he's reading he does so aloud, and when he's working on a math problem he calculates aloud. Jimmy has reflected on his need to talk and understands that he needs to control this tendency, stating that he will try to do so, "I do try to stop, but it's very hard for me." He also does his work more independently and is developing strategies to deal with frustration. Getting homework done is still a problem. In one session, Jimmy and Dr. G. talked about the impossibility of completing his assignments when Jimmy was in an upset state. Jimmy bet Dr. G. $20 that he could be upset and still finish his work. Smiling in session after session, he promised that he would be able to do it "next week." Thus, Jimmy has begun to understand that regulating emotions is important for attention, concentration, and productivity.

Jimmy has continued to make progress. On a trip with his family to England he visited other family members who had not seen him for a number of years. All family members commented on the changes that Jimmy had made. Jimmy's mother writes about her feelings about the process in a way that captures Jimmy's progress:

Jimmy began his journey with Dr. Ira Glovinsky when he was just six years old. Those initial visits were primarily diagnostic and evaluative and it was painfully evident Jimmy wanted no part of it. Very sporadically, over the next two years, he and Ira met. In most of the sessions, Ira encountered an angry, sullen, and extremely anxious little boy. While Jimmy balked at going, and once there, refused to speak, the process of therapy had inevitably been launched.

For the next year, Ira was still very much involved in Jimmy's life. He consulted with us about schooling, directing us to a psychiatrist for guidance through several medication trials and ultimately referred us to Dr. Gianni Faedda, a specialist in New York for expert consultation.

For the last 18 months, I have watched Jimmy develop an intense relationship with Ira and observed remarkable benefits of this therapeutic process. There are several elements in Jimmy's work with Ira that have contributed to the progress. The most significant has been my presence and involvement in his therapy sessions. So much of our progress has been made because I can take from therapy strategies and skills to apply at home. I feel capable of helping Jimmy self-monitor, problem solve, reflect, defuse anger, articulate feelings, and cope with obsessive-compulsive behaviors. Sometimes issues brought up in therapy are revisited during the week and talking about them helps Jimmy process it all.

Much of our early work involved getting to know and really understand my son. I often felt confused and intimidated by Jimmy's actions. His angry outbursts and loss of control overwhelmed me. I didn't know how to interpret or react to his behaviors. On the surface I saw an angry, hostile, and oppositional child out to get me. Those perceptions, of course shaped my responses. My anger and defensiveness kept me from becoming an effective parent.

I realize now that many of Jimmy's behaviors are actually defenses fueled by his tremendous anxiety and fiercely negative image of himself. Ira helped me to see what lay beneath. Knowing this, I am able to respond more effectively. I understand the connection between how I react to an episode and how it will play out—its duration, intensity, and outcome. I am able to accept, although it is painful, that parenting a bipolar child defies all traditional parenting strategies. Things that once made sense and were successful with my daughter just don't work. It's an entirely different arena and a whole new set of rules.

At times, I can use my participation in therapy to help steer the direction of a session. If issues occur during the week that I feel are important to talk out, I'm able to start the process of discussion. I can help fill in the blanks and provide the other perspective. I don't think Jimmy is ready to initiate this on his own quite yet. It will come eventually.

Parenting a bipolar child is incredibly challenging, and yet the role a parent takes is so absolutely fundamental to its successful management. It is the parents who are on the front line after the 45-minute therapy session ends. We're the ones who go home and work to hold everything together until the next appointment. When I leave a session with Jimmy, I feel empowered. I am learning to help my son help himself. Much of it is painful, a lot of it is stressful, and all of it is hard work.

However, it's the very strength of this relationship between parent and child that carries the most weight among the variables of what works, and what doesn't. Medications, teachers, schools, programs, even specialized ones, can only do so much. By sharing in Jimmy's therapy, it sends a powerful message to him that this isn't just HIS problem. That we're in this together has strengthened our relationship. He knows I'm on his side, I do want to help and that I love him very much.

In summary, the goals and strategies Dr. G. used in working with Jimmy came directly from Jimmy's developmental profile. The profile helped Dr. G. to see that Jimmy had been derailed at a very early stage of emotional functioning by his sensory sensitivities and the bombardment of his biology and emotions that affected his ability to develop a state of calm arousal. Unable to master this state, he was unable to master higher level developmental tasks of intimacy, engagement, and two-way communication. The developmental profile provided the information about where Dr. G. needed to focus his efforts. Without this map it would have been difficult to recognize Jimmy's profound pre-symbolic needs—needs unmet when he was not yet able to communicate them through symbols or words—because he was a boy of high intelligence and many words. Perhaps Dr. G. would have addressed him at too high a verbal level, mistakenly believing that because he had a large vocabulary he could understand abstract ideas and emotions. Clearly, he could not, and this disability contributed to failures to help him at home and at school. Jimmy's needs had to be addressed at a lower, pre-symbolic level before Dr. G. could slowly give him the tools to reach a higher functional level.

By using the developmental profile as a roadmap, Dr. G. was able to see how Jimmy's sensory needs contributed to his problems and to keep those needs in mind as he, Jimmy, and Jimmy's parents worked together. The profile also enabled Dr. G. to provide information to Jimmy's teachers based on what had emerged from his evaluation and their work together. For example, Jimmy's teacher was able to understand that his avoidance of work in school was, in part, related to a significant written expressive difficulty. Jimmy had genuine difficulty putting his ideas on paper. Thus, his misbehavior when he had to write was a sign that he was having trouble, not evidence of a defiant personality.

Jimmy's reactions have become more understandable, and he has been able to help his helpers by verbalizing more of his thoughts and feelings. The combination of his high intelligence, emotional sensitivity, and emerging reflectivity has made the work productive, and Jimmy has become more active in seeking out help that he needs. He is clearly able to recognize that his environment is filled with help and support, and although there continue to be rough times, it is no longer so frightening for him as when his therapy began.

The History of
Bipolar Disorder in Children

If you are the parent of a child who at times seems to be on an emotional roller coaster, you may wonder why we are including the history of bipolarity in this book. Who cares how children with cyclic mood patterns have been viewed and treated in the past, you might ask. My child is suffering and needs help now—isn't that all that matters? Yet the struggles that clinicians have today in diagnosing the disorder are very much a result of its history, and understanding that history may help parents to understand these struggles. Many parents experience the frustration of going from one disagreeing professional to another without finding the help they need for their child and wonder why. The answer is by no means simple, but part of it lies in the complicated manner in which diagnosis and treatment of bipolarity have evolved over time.

Mania and depression, referred to as *melancholia,* appeared in writings over a thousand years ago in classical Greece. Of course, the mania and melancholia that authors wrote about in ancient times were not exactly the same conditions that clinicians describe today, but their descriptions were similar and were grouped into large categories in the same way as disorders are today in the DSM-IV. *Mania* was often used as a general term for madness, although at times it was more specific and described "raving madness." *Melancholia* often referred to either "craziness" or "sadness," but it could also mean a more long-lasting fearfulness or sadness.

The ancients had some idea that these disorders might be connected, but only about 150 years ago were the two conditions identified as part of a cycling type of disorder. Dr. Stanley Jackson, in *Melancholia and Depression,* summarizes the relationship between mania and melancholia up to the Renaissance:

- The two conditions were considered together as "diseases of the head."

- They were grouped together as two chronic forms of madness.

- Few cases were seen as associated with fever.

- Mania was seen as a severe excited state and melancholia as a severe dejected state.

This view remained relatively unchanged throughout the sixteenth and seventeenth centuries, though an occasional author began to link mania with melancholia. By the eighteenth century, furthermore, an occasional case description sounded very much like what we would now describe as mania. For example, A. Crichton, in 1798, describes the case of a very young child:

On the 20th January, 1763, was brought to bed without any assistance, a male child who was raving mad. When he was brought to our workhouse, which was on the 24th, he possessed so much strength in his legs and arms, that four women could, at times, with difficulty restrain him. These paroxysms either ended in indescribable laughter for which no evident reason could be observed, or else he tore in anger every thing near him, clothes, linen, bed, furniture, even thread when he could get hold of it. We durst not allow him to be alone, otherwise he would get on the benches and table, and even attempt to climb up the walls.

In the American literature, we began to see some descriptions of manic behavior in the nineteenth century. T.C. Morison in 1848 wrote about a six-year-old girl who presented with mania:

When admitted to Bethelem Hospital, her conduct was violent and mischievious; striking those about her, tearing her clothes and destroying everything within her reach. She was generally incoherent in her speech—repeating any words she might hear in a monotonous voice, and without appearing to understand them, such as 'Poor thing, poor thing. . . .' She could not be induced to employ herself in any way, and was subject to violent and unaccountable outbursts of passion, in which she tore her clothes, and bit and scratched all who attempted to restrain her.

Terms such as "neurodevelopmental disorder" or "tactile sensitivity" were nowhere in the vocabulary of practitioners during those times; children with bipolar patterns were simply labeled as "mad" and often put away in "madhouses" with adults.

We know that many children in the early nineteenth century suffered from mental illness. For example, between 1815 and 1899, 1069 children and adolescents were admitted to Bethlem Royal Hospital, often referred to as "Bedlam." Over half of those admitted suffered from delusions, and there were many that were described as having some type of mania and/or melancholia.

Not until the 1850s were mania and depression finally wedded into a single cycling disorder, one moving into the other either directly, or perhaps separated by a period during which the patient appeared normal. Two French psychiatrists, Jules Baillarger (1809–1890) and Jean-Pierre Falret (1794–1870), working at the same hospital in France, Salpêtrière, each described a cycling-type illness that included mania and depression. Baillarger referred to it as *la folie à double forme*—double form madness—and Falret referred to *la folie circulaire*—circular madness. Not until the twentieth century was the argument regarding who should be credited resolved. When the verdict finally came in, the answer was that they both should.

Simultaneous with these developments in England, France, and America, exquisite descriptions of mania came out of Germany in the early 1900s. The work of Theodore Ziehen, a German clinician whose works almost disappeared until three contemporary clinicians, Christopher Bathage, Ira Glovinsky, and Ross Baldesserani recently rediscovered and wrote about his work, describes the disorder in terms remarkably similar to those we use today:

> The pathological mirth of mania differs only in degree from the natural zest of a healthy child. The flight of ideas in mania finds its counterpart in the normal vividness of the infantile association of ideas. The abnormal compulsion to move can hardly be differentiated from the gamboling of some healthy children. The pathological excesses of the maniacal child suggest at first almost always a regular disobedience. In order to be protected from such deceptions and diagnose the mania in time, the practitioner needs to observe that the latter almost always sets in rapidly: the contrast with the prior behavior of the child and sudden unmotivated transformation of the psychic demeanor give the best indications that the normal condition has been replaced by serious mental derangement. In addition, pathological absence of exhaustion and sleep set in as equally infallible symptoms. After having exhausted themselves, wild and healthy children tend to get tired and sleep well. This normal weariness and its normal compensation through sleep are missing during mania.

As the twentieth century progressed, however, few clinicians were willing to accept the diagnosis of bipolar disorder in children as legitimate. Some work on childhood bipolar patterns was conducted by small pockets of professionals who favored the diagnosis in this country in the 1930s, at the University of Michigan Children's Psychiatric Hospital, for example, but the disagreement was intense. Certain people who opposed the diagnosis had a great deal of influence in the field of psychiatry. For example, Charles Bradley, one of the key figures in child psychiatry in the 1940s, all but killed the diagnosis when he wrote that any professional who diagnosed a child with "manic-depression" (as it was called during that time) essentially needed more schooling. Bradley continued,

> It is likely that in the rare reported cases of manic psychoses in children that there may well have been confusion either in observation or interpretation of motor activity, impulsiveness, or other similar childhood symptoms, and attempts to fit the patient into an adult psychiatric classification which does not apply to children seems unwarranted. . . .

> Severe depressions are not seen in children. What effect puberty and maturity of the psyche as seen in later adolescence and adult life have on the capacity of the individual to develop symptoms either of mania or depression awaits further investigation. For the present it is best to avoid the diagnosis of manic-depressive psychosis or affective psychosis in children.

Bradley was correct in saying that we should not use adult classifications for children, and this is a major problem that we face today that interferes with correctly diagnosing childhood disturbances. But, he was wrong in trying to kill the diagnosis. A brief revival came about in the 1950s. John Campbell, a well-known psychiatrist, wrote about a number of children and adolescents who displayed manic behavior. However, Goliath slew David in the 1960s when E.J. Anthony and P. Scott decided to develop their own diagnostic classification system and made it all but impossible for a child to be diagnosed with manic-depression. In essence, if clinicians create enough criteria to exclude everyone, then the disorder no longer exists. During this period, clinicians still treated children who clearly evidenced mania, but these children did not have a home in any diagnostic system. Manic-depressive children became what Gaye Carlson now refers to as "diagnostically homeless."

Fortunately, there were professionals who would not give up. Two neurologists, W. Weinberg and R. Brumback, described some cases of manic behavior in children and Robert DeLong followed by using lithium with children with manic patterns. This was followed in 1978 by an article published by Gaye Carlson and Michael Strober. They introduced the idea that perhaps the reason mania was so rare in children was that it was misdiagnosed as schizophrenia. Elizabeth Weller, another pioneer in the field, further opened the door by investigating a number of historical cases and concluding that there was a higher degree of misdiagnosis.

Thus, where bipolar patterns in children are concerned, throughout history there have been believers and nonbelievers engaged in heated discussions that continue to the present time. The development of the *Diagnostic and Statistical Manual of the American Psychiatric Association* was an attempt to classify mental disorders categorically. Over the years of revision we have seen that the use of adult classifications for children is highly inappropriate. In one sense, Anthony and Scott's conclusions have been correct. There is increasing agreement that a classical pattern of mania as seen in adults—cycling through periods of high euphoria and expansive behavior to severe depression punctuated by periods of relative wellness—is exceedingly rare in young children. Meanwhile, in the words of Gaye Carlson, "There is no disputing the fact that a substantial number of preadolescent children have symptoms of mania, usually superimposed on a number of diverse developmental and psychiatric conditions."

We are in agreement with this, but we see the current investigations of these patterns as being constricted by the same rules that have been used throughout history. We feel that in order to understand and to treat these children, we must go beyond categorical thinking and look at these children through a "biopsychosocial" lens.

Children and Babies with Mood Swings

Key Events in the History of Childhood Bipolar Disorder

Ancient Greece	Mania seen as a general term for madness or, more specifically, "raving madness; "melancholia" used to denote sadness as well depression.
Pre-Renaissance Europe	Mania = severe excited state; melancholia = severe dejected state. These were seen as two separate disorders.
18th century Europe	Occasional case descriptions of children with manic symptoms.
19th century Europe	Children with mental illnesses admitted to "madhouses" and America along with adults; many described as having mania or melancholia.
1850s—France (Salpêtrière)	Mania and melancholia linked as a single disorder by Baillager (la folie á double forme) and Falret (la folie circulaire).
Early 1900s—Germany	Ziehen's detailed descriptions of mania.
1910–1970s—Europe and America	Majority of psychiatrists rejected manic depression as a diagnosis for children, leaving these children "diagnostically homeless."
1970s—America	More clinicians began accepting the diagnosis. De Long treated with bipolar children with lithium; Carlson and Strober hypothesized that these children had been misdiagnosed with schizophrenia, a theory supported by Weller's investigations of historical cases.
2007	Diagnosis of bipolar disorder in children more widely accepted, but remains controversial and framed primarily in biological terms rather than as a biopsychosocial disorder in which the child's developmental level and environment play a significant role. DSM-IV criteria for bipolar disorder increasingly seen as inappropriate for children.

We see children as evidencing a pattern of behavior that is marked by sensory processing challenges, challenges in back-and-forth interactions with caregivers and other adults, and trouble representing their emotions mentally so that when they experience an emotion it is immediately discharged in an action mode.

As long as we continue to use lists of symptoms, we keep the door open to mis-diagnosis and consequent mis-treatment. We will continue to underdiagnose, overdiagnose, and misdiagnose. And, in so doing, we present a major danger that is severe today, i.e., prescribing the wrong medications and the wrong treatment.

In contrast, by using a biopsychosocial lens and focusing on the patterns that these children present, we have the opportunity to focus on each child's individual pattern of strengths and weaknesses and to design a treatment program that is unique to each child's individual needs. This is the focus of this book.

This brief historical chapter highlights important points of time in the development of the concept of bipolar disorder. Those who are interested in a more in-depth description of the history might want to look at the historical chapter in our previous book, *Bipolar Patterns in Children.*

What Current Research Tells Us about Bipolar Patterns in Children

Knowledge is power. Parents of children with extreme mood cycles who are informed about the latest research findings can be powerful advocates for their children. Their knowledge enables them to discuss what they've learned with the professionals who treat or educate their children. Often these professionals do not have expertise in a single diagnostic area like mood disorders, much less as specific a condition such as bipolar disorder. Research results are most often presented in journals not typically read by educators, pediatricians, or other helping professionals.

Sitting in on Individual Education Planning Committee (IEPC) meetings with professionals and parents, we have had the opportunity to watch what happens when a parent educates school personnel. For example, the mother of one child we treated for bipolar patterns made notebooks for each of the professionals who worked with her child, notebooks which included a section on research. The parent received a lot of positive feedback from the educators for sharing this information; they felt that the research information offered them specific ideas about areas that could be addressed in school. The educational plan complemented and supported the treatment plan that the family's therapist had developed for the family at home, which also included plans for work in school and in therapy sessions.

Notwithstanding the long history of childhood bipolar disorder described, research in this area is still in its infancy. The research covers a number of different areas, and new results are being gathered every day. Thus, in this book, rather than trying to present the latest findings in detail—findings that may be out of date by the time this book goes to press—we merely try to map out the major areas of inquiry and indicate the kinds of questions researchers are currently asking about bipolar patterns in children.

A primary goal of present-day researchers is to develop a way of describing bipolar patterns that covers those children who do not meet the narrow, rigid criteria described in the *Diagnostic and Statistical Manual of Mental Disorders (DSM-IV-TR)* currently being used by mental health practitioners. Many children with bipolar patterns do not meet the diagnostic criteria either because they do not display episodes of mania for the duration required to make the diagnosis (seven days) or because they do not evidence what we call the cardinal symptoms of bipolar disorder: euphoria (emotional highs) or grandiosity (inaccurately inflating one's sense of power, self-worth, and importance).

At present, we are unsure whether bipolar disorder is a single condition that changes with development from childhood to adulthood; a totally different childhood condition in the way juvenile diabetes is totally different from adult-onset type II diabetes; a subtype coming under the umbrella of a more general disorder; or a temperamental variation that may not be predictive of any later disturbance. Current research is exploring all of these possibilities.

Other research is devoted to clarifying terminology. For example, if "grandiosity" is a cardinal symptom of bipolar disorder, then how do we define it in childhood? Where do we draw the line between the child who says he or she is the smartest child in the class and the child who truly believes that he or she could teach better than the teacher? What about the child who enjoys dressing up as a super-hero? How do we differentiate the child who knows he is pretending from the child who won't be stopped from accomplishing a "Mission Impossible"? Defining terminology is an important area of research that is needed if we are to make accurate diagnoses.

Another area of research relates to how we make the diagnosis of bipolar disorder. This is a highly contentious area because children with bipolar disorder often behave differently in different settings. It is not unusual for a child with a bipolar pattern to do well in a school setting, but tear the house apart after school is over. Similarly, children may behave differently when different adults in their lives have different thresholds for tolerating their behavior. In one situation, for example, grandparents reported that they had absolutely no difficulty with a child who was wreaking havoc at home. I asked the parents to bring videotapes of the child's interactions with the grandparents. When we looked at these videos, we saw that the grandparents were letting the child control everything and making no attempt to set limits. Thus, when professionals evaluate these children there is often an "informer variance" that may lead to differing diagnoses. We need to develop tools that provide consistency across informants, and we are far from having these tools at this point.

Medication is a serious area for research. There is a lot of controversy about the use of antidepressants with children with patterns of both increased activity and increased mood intensity. We are not sure whether these medications should be avoided because they may activate a child who is predisposed to bipolar disorder. However, there may be children who become over-active and even manic in response to any medication. Gaye Carlson, a senior investigator in the area of pediatric bipolar disorder, recently described a child who was treated with asthma medication and developed manic symptoms in response to almost every medication he was given. This child was not even being treated for a mood disorder. Should anti-depressants be avoided because they are toxic for children with bipolar disorder, or do some children happen to be allergic to medication? How should we use anti-depressants with children with extreme mood cycles?

A similar controversy exists for stimulants. These medications are used to treat Attention Deficit/Hyperactivity Disorder, which overlaps significantly with bipolar disorder. The use of stimulants with children with bipolar patterns often destabilizes them. At the same time, because Attention Deficit and bipolar disorder dance together in over ninety per cent of cases, the AD/HD component must be addressed. Research is important in helping us to resolve these dilemmas.

Along with trying to find better ways to define, diagnose, and treat bipolar patterns in children, researchers are looking for indicators that a given child is likely to develop adult-type bipolar disorder. How important is family history in making the diagnosis of bipolar disorder? Does a family history of bipolar disorder increase the risk of developing bipolar disorder? How about early childhood symptoms and diagnoses? Recent research has shown that depression in early childhood is often a harbinger of bipolar disorder in adolescence. When we see a very young child with depressive symptoms, should we be thinking about preventive methods of treating that child that will protect him or her from developing the disorder?

Research in the area of pediatric bipolar disorder is also looking into the areas of neuropsychology, social neuroscience, neuroimaging, and neurodevelopmental functioning. For example, a recent neuropsychological study showed that children with bipolar disorder had more trouble shifting their attention set and more problems with visual-spatial memory than healthy children had. Methodological problems make these results tentative and possibly difficult to generalize. However, the results relating to attention shift do seem to fit with parents' reports of their children being unable to move easily from one activity to another. Also, children with visual-spatial memory problems may have difficulty creating a pictorial map of their environments. They may forget such things as how to get from one class to the next class within the school environment.

The social neuroscience area is a recent addition to neuroscience, and studies are beginning to emerge in which children with bipolar disorder are being compared to children with other psychiatric diagnoses. For example, a recent study comparing children with bipolar disorder to children with anxiety disorders and to healthy children found that those with bipolar disorder had the most difficulty interpreting children's facial expressions of sadness, happiness, and fearfulness. They interpreted all these facial expressions as anger. They did not have the same difficulty interpreting adult facial expressions, however. This is consistent with our observations that children with mood instability often misinterpret other children's facial or gestural communication and quickly react aggressively, without holding back to evaluate the situation, believing that the other children are going to attack or assault them.

Many other studies are being carried out in this area, but at this point there are many questions relating to the purity of samples, the fact that children are on different medications while being evaluated, and the small size of study samples. Therefore, at this point in time the generalizability of studies must still be studied.

In recent decades, new neuro-imaging techniques have enabled researchers to investigate brain functioning and treatment effects in different populations, including bipolar disorder. However, as with neuropsychological studies, the results of these studies are preliminary. For example, evidence is accumulating of white matter hyperintensities in both higher and lower regions of the brain and of some brain structures that have been associated with emotionality—the part of the brain's limbic system called the amygdala, for example—being smaller in children evidencing bipolar patterns. However, these results are difficult to interpret at this point because the findings are very general and are associated with a number of different disease processes such as inflammation, reduced blood flow to the arteries of the brain, and changes in the white fatty sheath that covers neurons.

A Pilot Study on the Sensory Profiles of Children with Bipolar Patterns of Mood Dysregulation

We have been conducting preliminary research regarding concepts presented in Chapter 4. Our interest is in exploring the underlying sensory patterns in children whose symptoms fit bipolar patterns.

To try to see how sensory and bipolar patterns fit together, we recently conducted a small pilot study to investigate "Sensory Profiles" (results of a parent questionnaire developed by Winnie Dunn that evaluates how a child processes sensory input and how this processing affects the child's performance and daily life) of children between the ages of three and ten years who had both significant family histories of bipolar disorder and diagnosis of early-onset bipolar patterns themselves. The children had each received the diagnosis after two independent evaluations by a psychologist and a child psychiatrist who specialize in this disorder. Parents provided comprehensive, three-generation (child, parents, and grandparents) family histories in which they often spontaneously reported a family history of bipolar disorder or manic-depression. We also interviewed children, observed them in play with their parents, and administered psychological tests. Parents filled out child-behavior questionnaires concerning the development of symptoms from infancy to the present time.

The Sensory Profile consists of 125 items separated into three sections: Sensory Processing, Modulation, and Behavioral and Emotional Responses. The Sensory section assesses the child's responses to auditory, visual, vestibular, touch, multisensory, and oral sensory processing; the Modulation section looks at the child's ability to regulate neural messages by facilitating or inhibiting different types of responses; and the Behavioral and Emotional Responses section reflects a child's behavioral outcomes of sensory processing.

The findings of this preliminary study support our hypothesis that children with bipolar patterns evidence sensory processing challenges of the type we have previously described. Their scores showed significant differences in Vestibular Processing (response to movement stimulation, items such as "seeks all kinds of movement activities and this interferes with daily routines"). They also showed hypersensitivities to sound and touch as well as trouble with oral (taste, mouth movements) and multisensory processing. In addition, the children appeared to have problems with modulation in the presence of intense sensory input. Instead of becoming cautious, as many children do who are overresponsive to sensations, the children with mood swings become active and sensory-seeking, for example, reacting emotionally to loud noises, tactile discomfort, or multisensory input and often engaging in tantrums, fights, and other extreme behaviors. This supports our hypothesis that children with mood swings tend to evidence a unique regulatory-sensory processing pattern which we described in our earlier book and which was recently described in the new *ICDL-Diagnostic Manual for Infancy and Early Childhood*. This pattern involves both sensory over-responsivity and sensory-seeking. (The child in a sense keeps overwhelming himself.)

This small study represents a first attempt at exploring some of the underlying sensory and modulation factors that may underlie the irritability, intensity, stimulus craving, and regulation difficulties that characterize the behaviors of young children with bipolar patterns. The results indicate the need for further studies undertaken on a much larger scale.

Research Findings as a Window of Opportunity

New research is helping us to understand which children are more vulnerable to developing bipolar patterns. We are learning to watch for early developmental patterns that include sensory hyper-reactivity and irritability together with craving sensory input and related mood "ups and downs." We are more aware of the effects of stress and life events on a child with these patterns and the effects on their capacity to learn to regulate their mood with a parent or parents who have mood instability themselves. We are learning that changing moods tend to run in families, and that when a very young child evidences depression, this may be an early sign to attend to. We are also learning that severe disruptive behavior in young children, in the context of a family history of bipolar disorder, may require special attention.

An understanding of what we should look out for leads directly to strategies to prevent further exacerbation of these patterns. By identifying the early signs of bipolar patterns, we may be able to interrupt the development of the processes that are so disruptive to the child, the family, the school, and the community.

Conclusion

In this book, we have discussed children with mood swings, particularly children now receiving the diagnosis of bipolar disorder, using a developmental, biopsychosocial model which we called the Developmental, Individual-Difference, Relationship-Based (DIR) model. This model allows us to look at the earliest stages of a child's personality development prior to the unfolding of language and to consider how biological and sensory differences as well as interactions with caregivers within a particular environment contribute to this development.

Emotional regulation emerges from experiences prior to the unfolding of language. Through the warm, non-verbal back-and-forth chains of interaction that an infant has with his or her caregivers, the child shifts from using others to help control his or her emotions and behaviors to regulating them with self-control. What starts as outside control develops into internal control. The child moves from an "action mode" mode to a self-reflective "symbolic mode" where wishes and feelings are placed into words rather than acted out in actions. Children who have difficulty controlling their emotions have not developed or are unable to express themselves in words and symbols. Wishes and feelings are discharged through actions or through bodily descriptions, rather than in feeling words such as "I feel mad!"

The challenge with children who are stuck in an action mode is to help them to move to a higher level of functioning where they can use feeling words. We must also help children to express emotions in specific rather than black-or-white terms, as in everything being either great or terrible, for example. We must help children to see that there are shades of gray.

Using a developmental model enables parents to create developmentally appropriate experiences at home, and teachers to develop age-appropriate experiences at school that are geared to the child's specific functional developmental challenges, such as the inability to fully represent feelings and wishes and regulate interactions, as well as the child's particular sensory processing and motor profiles.

In this book we also formulated a novel hypothesis about the possible contribution of sensory processing differences to mood dysregulation in children with bipolar-type patterns. These differences consist of an unusual processing pattern in which the child is over-responsive to sound, touch, or both and also craves sensory stimulation, particularly movement. This sensory-craving is usually associated with high activity levels and agitated and impulsive behavior. Furthermore, when these children are overloaded with stimuli, they cannot self-regulate like typical children. Their inner emotional thermostats don't return to a calm set point, but rather move to an even higher level of dysregulation. In addition, their interactions with others lack the smooth back-and-forth emotional exchanges that can be likened to a comfortable tennis volley where each partner hits the ball in a way that enables his or her partner to comfortably hit it back without straining. Finally, these children do not evidence the personality organization in which sharing ideas and emotional thinking have been mastered.

We have seen that family patterns can either intensify the dysregulated patterns or moderate them and help the child cope more efficiently. Our hope is that the model we have described will help parents and professionals to be more attuned to the particular challenges that underlie their children's behavior in their daily interactions and to use some of the strategies and techniques we have described to help their children begin to gain control over the cyclic ups and downs of their own emotions.

References

American Psychiatric Association. (1987). *Diagnostic and statistical manual for mental disorders.* (3rd ed., revised). Washington, D.C.

American Psychiatric Association. (1994). *Diagnostic and statistical manual for mental disorders.* (4th ed.). Washington, D.C.

American Psychiatric Association. (2000). *Diagnostic and statistical manual for mental disorders.* (4th ed., revised). Washington, D.C.

Anthony, E. J., & Scott, P. (1960). Manic-depressive psychosis in childhood. *Journal of Child Psychology and Psychiatry, 1,* 53–72.

Baethge, C., Glovinsky, I., & Baldessarini, R. (2004). Manic-depressive illness in children: An early twentieth-century view by Theodor Ziehen (1862–1950). *History of Psychiatry, 15,* 201–226.

Baldessarini, R. (2001). (personal communication).

Bowlby, J. (1951). Maternal Care and Mental Health. *WHO Monograph,* 51. Geneva: World Health Organization.

Bradley, C. (1945). Psychoses in children. In N. Lewis & B. Pacella (Eds.), *Modern Trends in Child Psychiatry* (pp. 135–154). New York: International Universities Press.

Campbell, J. D. (1952). Manic-depressive psychosis in children: Report of 18 cases. *Journal of Nervous Mental Disorders, 116,* 426–439.

Carlson, G. A. (1983). Bipolar affective disorders in children and adolescents. In D. P. Cantwell & G. A. Carlson (Eds.), *Affective disorders in children and adolescents: An update* (pp. 61–83). New York: Spectrum Press.

Carlson, G. A. (1995). Identifying prepubertal mania: Commentary. *Journal of the American Academy of Child and Adolescent Psychiatry, 34,* 750–753.

Carlson, G. A., & Fahim, F. (1998). "Georgie." *Journal of Affective Disorders, 51,* 195–198.

Carlson, G. A., & Goodwin, F. (1973). The stages of mania. *Archives of General Psychiatry, 28*, 221–228.

Carlson, G. A., & Kashani, J. (2002). Mood disorders. *Child and Adolescent Psychiatric Clinics of North America, 11*, 3, xv–xvii.

Crichton, A., Sir. (1798). An inquiry into the nature and origin of mental derangement: Comprehending a concise system of physiology and pathology of the human mind and a history of passions and their effect. London: Printed for T. Cadell, Jr. and W. Davies.

Crichton-Browne, J. (1860). Psychical disease in early life. *Journal of Mental Science, 6*, 284–320.

DeLong, G. R. (1990). Lithium treatment and bipolar disorders in childhood. *North Carolina Medical Journal, 51(4)*, 152–154.

Dunn, W. (1999). *Sensory profile, user's manual.* San Antonio, TX: The Psychological Corporation.

Dunn, W., & Brown, C. (1997). Factor analysis on the sensory profile from a national sample of children without disabilities. *American Journal of Occupational Therapy, 51*(7), 490–495.

Erikson, E. H. (1959). *Identity and the life cycle: Selected papers.* New York: International Universities Press.

Freud, A. (1965). *Normality and pathology in childhood: Assessments of development.* New York: International Universities Press.

Freud, S. (1962). *Three essays on the theory of sexuality.* New York: Avon Books.

Freud, S. (1963). *The sexual identity of children.* New York: Collier Books.

Furth, H. G., & Wachs, W. (1975). Thinking goes to school: Piaget's theory in practice. London: Oxford University Press.

Greenspan, J., & Greenspan, S. I. (2002). Functional Emotional Developmental Questionnaire (FEDQ) for infancy and childhood: A preliminary report on the questions and their clinical meaning. *Journal on Developmental and Learning Disorders, 6*, 71–116.

Greenspan, S. I. (1979). Intelligence and adaptation: An integration of psycho-analytic and Piagetian developmental psychology. *Psychological Issues, XII,* 3/4. New York: International Universities Press.

Greenspan, S. I. (1989). *The development of the ego: Implications for personality theory, psychopathology, and the psychotherapeutic process.* New York: International Universities Press.

Greenspan, S. I. (1992). *Infancy and early childhood: The practice of clinical assessment and intervention with emotional and developmental challenges.* Madison, CT: International Universities Press.

Greenspan, S. I. (1997). *Developmentally based psychotherapy.* Madison, CT: International Universities Press.

Greenspan, S. I. (1997). *The growth of the mind and the endangered origins of intelligence.* Reading, MA: Addison Wesley Longman.

Greenspan, S. I. (2001). The affect diathesis hypothesis: The role of emotions in the core deficit in autism and the development of intelligence and social skills. *Journal of Developmental and Learning Disorders, 5,* 1–45.

Greenspan, S. I., DeGangi, G. A., & Wieder, S. (2001). *The Functional Emotional Assessment Scale (FEAS) for Infancy & Early Childhood: Clinical & research applications.* Bethesda, MD: Interdisciplinary Council on Developmental and Learning Disorders.

Greenspan, S. I., & Lewis, N. B. (1999). *Building healthy minds: The six experiences that create intelligence and emotional growth in babies and young children.* Cambridge, MA: Perseus Publishing.

Greenspan, S. I., & Lourie, R. S. (1981). Developmental structuralist approach to the classification of adaptive and pathologic personality organizations: Infancy and Early Childhood. *Journal of the American Psychiatric Association, 138,* 725–735.

Greenspan, S. I., & Salmon, J. (1995). *The challenging child: Understanding, raising, and enjoying the five "difficult" types of children.* Reading, MA: Addison Wesley.

Greenspan, S. I., & Salmon, J. (1993). *Playground politics: Understanding the emotional life of your school-age child.* Reading, MA: Addison Wesley.

Greenspan, S. I., & Shanker, S. (2003). *The evolution of intelligence: How language, consciousness, and social groups come about.* Reading, MA: Perseus Books.

Greenspan, S. I., & Wieder, S. (1997). Developmental patterns and outcomes in infants and children with disorders in relating and communicating: A chart review of 200 cases of children with autistic spectrum diagnoses. *Journal of Developmental and Learning Disorders, 1,* 87–141.

Greenspan, S. I., & Wieder, S. (1998). *The child with special needs: Encouraging intellectual and emotional growth.* Reading, MA: Perseus Books.

Greenspan, S. I., & Wieder, S. (1999). A functional developmental approach to autism spectrum disorders. *Journal of the Association for Persons with Severe Handicaps, 24,* 147–161.

Greenspan, S. I., Wieder, S., Lieberman, A., Nover, R., Lourie, R., & Robinson, M. (1987). Infants in multirisk families: Case studies in preventive intervention. *Clinical Infant Reports.* New York: International Universities Press.

Jackson, S. (1990). *Melancholia and depression: From Hippocratic times to modern times.* New Haven: Yale University Press.

Kohut, H. (1971). *The analysis of self: A systematic approach to the psychoanalytic treatment of narcissistic personality disorders.* New York: International Universities Press.

Mahler, M. S., Pine, F., & Bergman, A. (1975). *The psychological birth of the human infant: Symbiosis and individuation.* New York: Basic Books.

Morison, T. C. (1848). A case of mania in a child six years old. *Journal of Psychological Medicine, 1,* 317–318.

Weinberg, W. A., & Brumback, R. A. (1976). Mania in childhood: Case studies and literature review. *American Journal of Disorders in Children, 130,* 380–385.

Weller, E. B., Weller, R. A., & Fristad, M. A. (1995). Bipolar disorders in children: Misdiagnosis, underdiagnosis, and future directions. *Journal of the American Academy of Child and Adolescent Psychiatry, 34,* 709–714.

Weller, E. B., Weller, R. A., Tucker, S. G., & Fristad, M. A. (1986). Mania in prepubertal children: Has it been underdiagnosed? *Journal of Affective Disorders, 11*, 1, 51–154.

Winnicott, D. W. (1931). *Clinical notes on the disorders of childhood.* London: Heineman.

Ziehen, T. G. (1917). *Die geisteskrankheiten des kindersalters.* Berlin: Van Reuther & Richard. [Federhofer, K. Trans.].